BANJO *Listen & Learn*
HOMESPUN MUSIC INSTRUCTION

Tony Trischka

20 Easy Banjo Solos

Play Along with a Master Picker

Featuring a Comprehensive Audio Lesson on CD

With Dede Wyland, Rhythm Guitar

Cover Photo by Greg Heisler
Audio Editor: Ted Orr
Mastered by: Ted Orr at
Nevessa Productions, Woodstock, N.Y.

ISBN 0-7935-7061-1

Homespun Tapes

EXCLUSIVELY DISTRIBUTED BY

HAL•LEONARD CORPORATION
7777 W. BLUEMOUND RD. P.O. BOX 13819 MILWAUKEE, WI 53213

© 1996 HOMESPUN TAPES LTD.
BOX 694
WOODSTOCK, NY 12498-0694
All Rights Reserved

No part of this publication may be reproduced in any form or by any means
without the prior written permission of the Publisher.

Visit Hal Leonard on the internet at http://www.halleonard.com
Visit Homespun Tapes on the internet at http://www.homespuntapes.com

BANJO Listen & Learn
HOMESPUN MUSIC INSTRUCTION

Tony TRISCHKA TEACHES
20 Easy Banjo Solos

Table of Contents

PAGE	CD TRACK	
	1	Intro Music—"Shortenin' Bread"
4	2	Introduction
5	3	Tuning Pitches

"Shortenin' Bread"

PAGE	CD TRACK	
5	4	Lesson Explanation
	5	"Shortenin' Bread"
	6	Instruction
6	7	Slow Version
	8	More Instruction

"Ground Hog"

PAGE	CD TRACK	
6	9	Lesson Explanation
	10	"Ground Hog"
	11	Instruction
	12	Slow Version

"Shady Grove"

PAGE	CD TRACK	
7	13	Lesson Explanation
	14	"Shady Grove" (1st Version)
	15	Slow Version
	16	"Shady Grove" (2nd Version)
	17	Instruction and Slow Version

"Train 45"

PAGE	CD TRACK	
8	18	Lesson Explanation and "Train 45"
	19	Slow Version
	20	Fast Version in "B"

"Sally Johnson"

PAGE	CD TRACK	
9	21	Lesson Explanation & "Sally Johnson"
	22	Instruction
	23	Slow Version

"Wildwood Flower"

PAGE	CD TRACK	
10	24	"Wildwood Flower"
	25	Instruction
	26	Slow Version

"Roll in My Sweet Baby's Arms"

PAGE	CD TRACK	
11	27	"Roll in My Sweet Baby's Arms"
	28	Slow Version & Instruction

"Pretty Polly"

PAGE	CD TRACK	
12	29	Tuning and Lesson Explanation
	30	"Pretty Polly"
13	31	Instruction
	32	Slow Version

"Nine Pound Hammer"

PAGE	CD TRACK	
14	33	"Nine Pound Hammer
	34	Instruction
	35	Slow Version
	36	Instruction

This book contains music examples and all of the instructional songs from the CD, and are labeled with track icons (◆) for the ease of locating the corresponding tracks. The remaining tracks listed here contain detailed explanation and instruction for these songs.

PAGE	CD TRACK	
		"Sitting on Top of the World"
15	37	"Sitting on Top of the World"
	38	Slow Version
	39	Instruction
		"John Henry"
16	40	"John Henry"
	41	Lesson Explanation
	42	Slow Version
	43	Instruction
		"Little Lisa Jane"
17	44	"Little Liza Jane"
	45	Instruction
	46	Slow Version
18	47	Instruction
		"Casey Jones"
18	48	"Casey Jones"
	49	Instruction
		"Little Maggie"
19	50	"Little Maggie"
	51	Instruction
	52	Slow Version
	53	Instruction
		"Back Up and Push"
20	54	"Back Up and Push"
21	55	Instruction
	56	Slow Version

PAGE	CD TRACK	
		"Red Wing"
21	57	"Red Wing"
22	58	Instruction
	59	Slow Version
		"Little Rabbit"
23	60	"Little Rabbit"
24	61	Instruction
	62	Slow Version
		"Uncle Joe"
25	63	"Uncle Joe"
	64	Instruction
		"Alabama Jubilee"
26	65	"Alabama Jubilee"
27	66	Instruction
	67	Slow Version
		"Cumberland Gap"
28	68	"Cumberland Gap"
	69	Tuning Explanation & Instruction
	70	Slow Version
	71	Outro
29		Banjo Notation Legend
30		A Selected Discography

CD instruction makes it easy! Find the section of the lesson you want with the press of a finger; play that segment over and over until you've mastered it; easily skip over parts you've already mastered—no clumsy rewinding or fast-forwarding to find your spot; listen with the best possible audio fidelity; follow along track-by-track with the book.

◆1 ◆2 Introduction

Welcome to *Easy Banjo Solos*. These are some of my favorite tunes—all bluegrass standards, with perhaps the exception of "Casey Jones," a song I grew up with and decided to include after having John Hartford tell me it was one that Earl Scruggs liked to play.

The purpose of this package is two-fold: First, to enhance your own enjoyment of the banjo when playing by yourself, second, to act as a repertoire extender if you're picking with others. You'll find fiddle tunes such as "Sally Johnson," "Little Rabbit," and "Uncle Joe," as well as breaks for bluegrass "hits" like "Nine Pound Hammer," "Sitting on Top of the World," and "Shady Grove."

Even though I intended this to be a repertoire builder rather than a strictly instructional aid, you should keep your eyes open for licks and ideas which can be applied to other tunes. Most of the pieces are in standard G tuning. "Pretty Polly" and "Cumberland Gap" are exceptions, so please pay attention to their indicated tunings.

I recommend that you listen to the accompanying CD (or other banjo music, for that matter) even when you're separated from your instrument (in your car, or walkman while you're jogging, etc.). If you can get the music in your ears, you'll find your learning curve will be greatly accelerated.

Good luck and enjoy!

Tony Trischka

◆3 G Tuning:

① = D
② = B
③ = G
④ = D
⑤ = G

◆4 The first tune we will be doing is "Shortenin' Bread." I'll play it first, then we'll pick it apart, slow it down and talk about some of the details in it.

◆5 Shortenin' Bread

G tuning: GDGBD
(5th - 1st)
Key of G

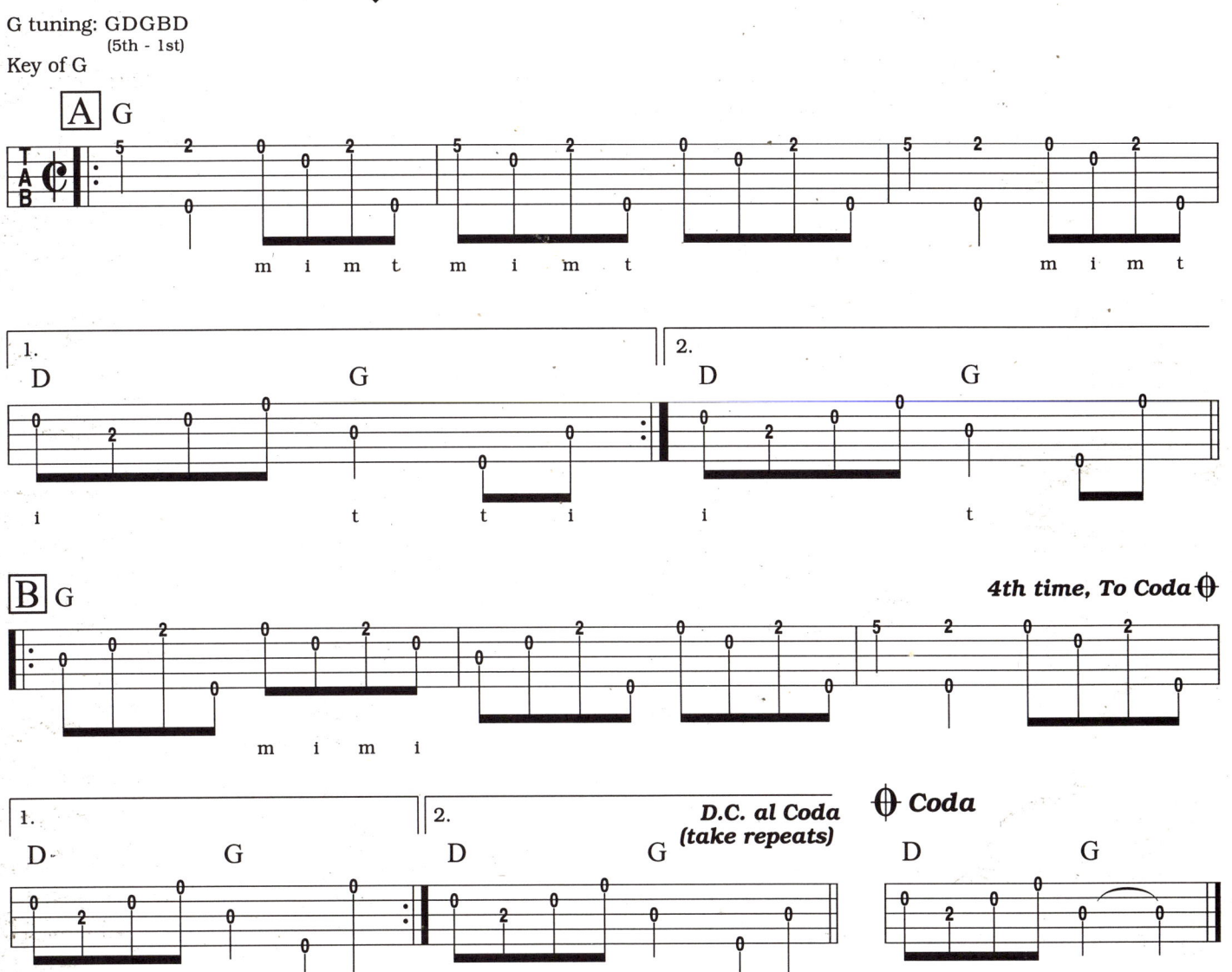

There are a couple of musical terms that may not be familiar to you that I should explain. Notice the **D.C. al Coda** marking in the second ending of part B. This indicates that you go back to the beginning of the tune (and in this case *take repeats*) and play until you see **To Coda** ⊕. At that point, jump to the measure marked **Coda** ⊕ to end the tune.

◆6 Use the pinky of your left hand to fret the first note located on the first string, fifth fret. The following note will be played with your first finger at the second fret.

7 Now I'll play parts A and B of "Shortenin' Bread" a little slower. With a little practice, you should soon be able to play along.

8 The m - i - m - t roll that appears in the first and third measures tends to be one of the more difficult right hand techniques. Practice this roll several times by itself and it will become easier to play.

9 Here is a fun song that I hope you enjoy!

10 Groundhog

G tuning: GDGBD
Key of G

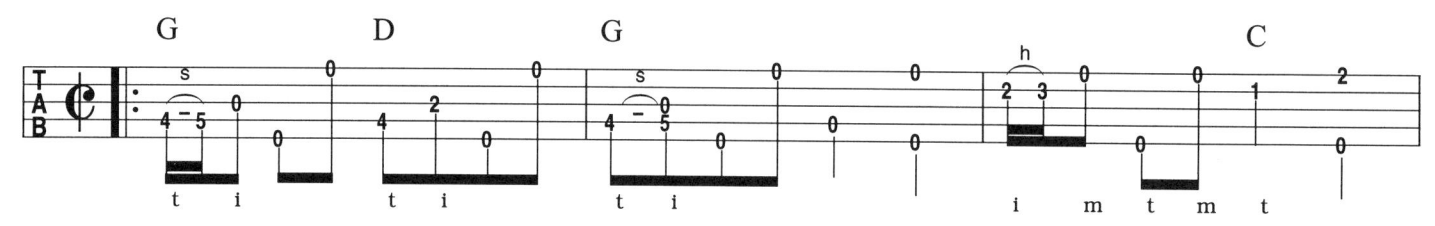

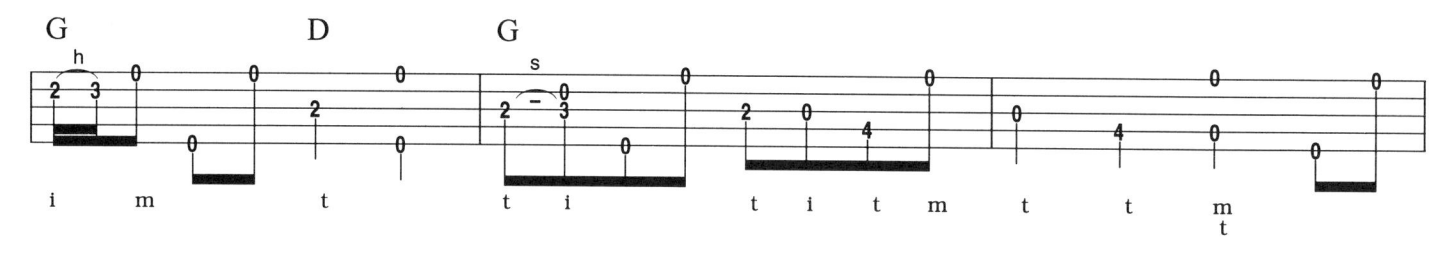

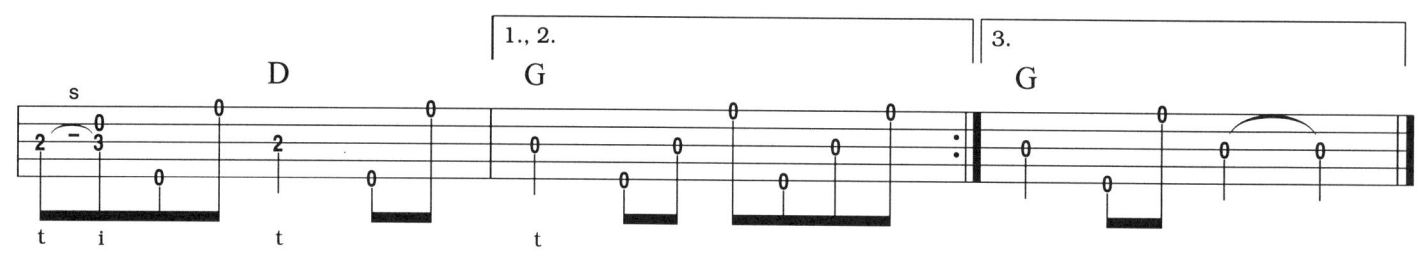

11 In this song I've incorporated the "Reno Technique" in which you have consecutive notes played on the same string. This occurs in the second line, second measure. Here you'll pick the first note with your thumb and the following note with your index finger.

12 Now I'll play "Ground Hog" once through a little slower. Try playing along!

13 ▸ Here are two versions of "Shady Grove." The first version is in the traditional bluegrass style while the second version is more of a folky rendition with fancy chords.

◆ **14** Shady Grove
(1st Version)

G tuning: GDGBD
Key of G

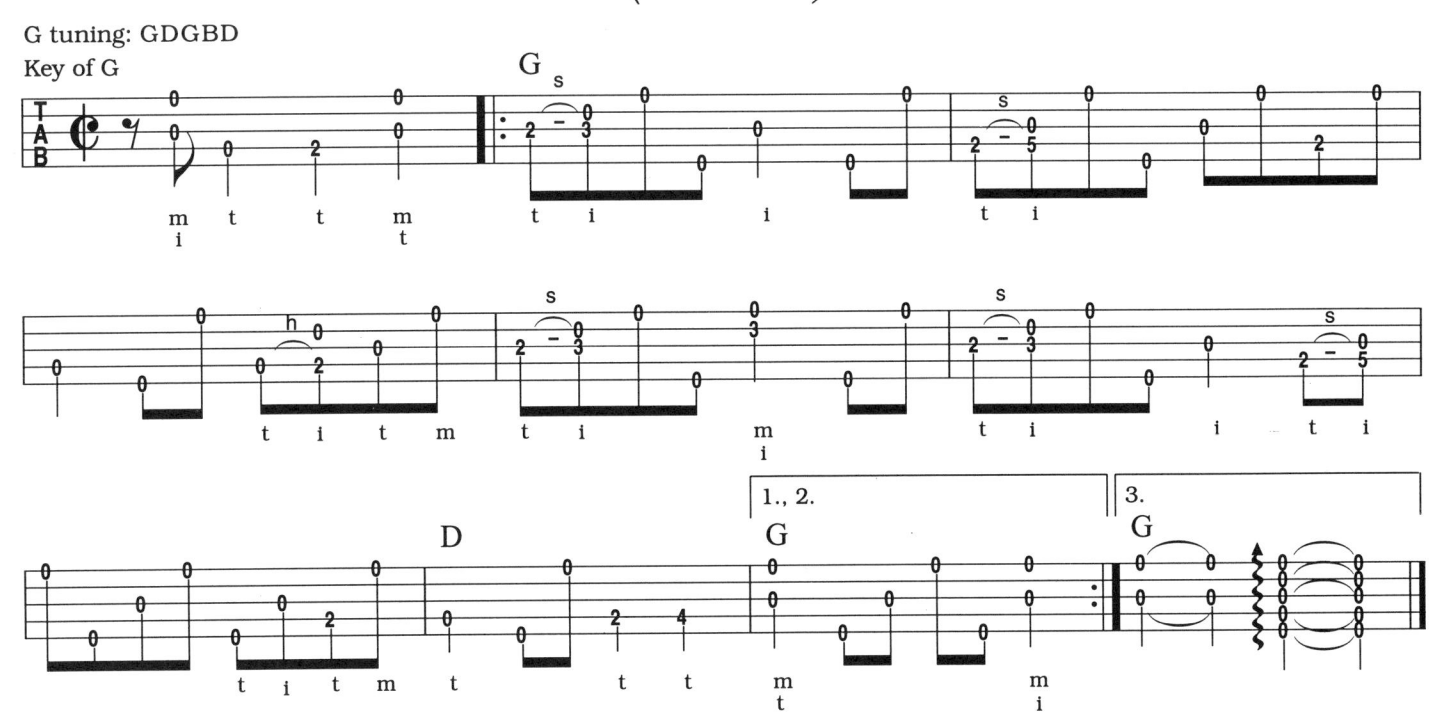

15 ▸ Now I'll play the first version once through slowly.

◆ **16** Shady Grove
(2nd Version)

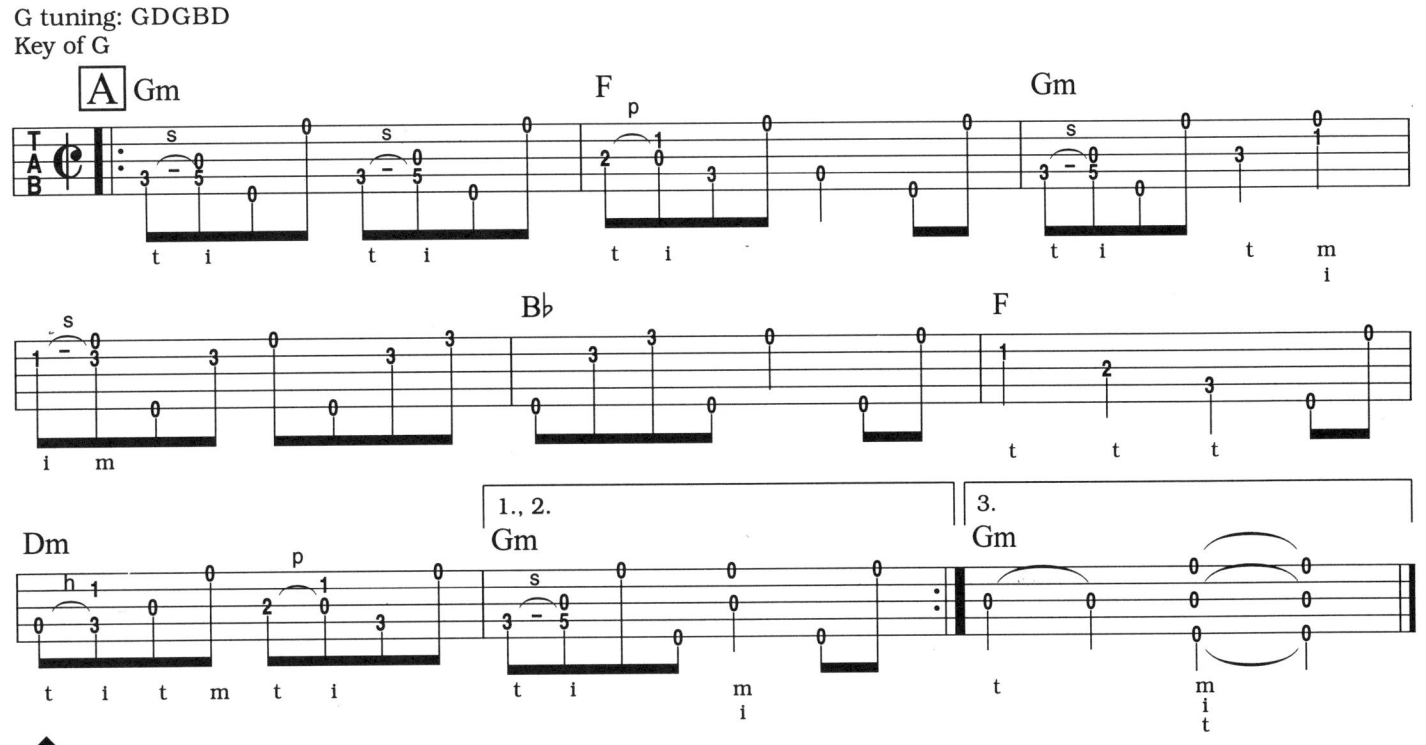

G tuning: GDGBD
Key of G

17 ▸ Make sure that you avoid picking the second string open-B note: B is the major third of a G chord. We'll want to play B♭ (the flatted third) on the fourth string, third fret for our Gm chords.

Train 45

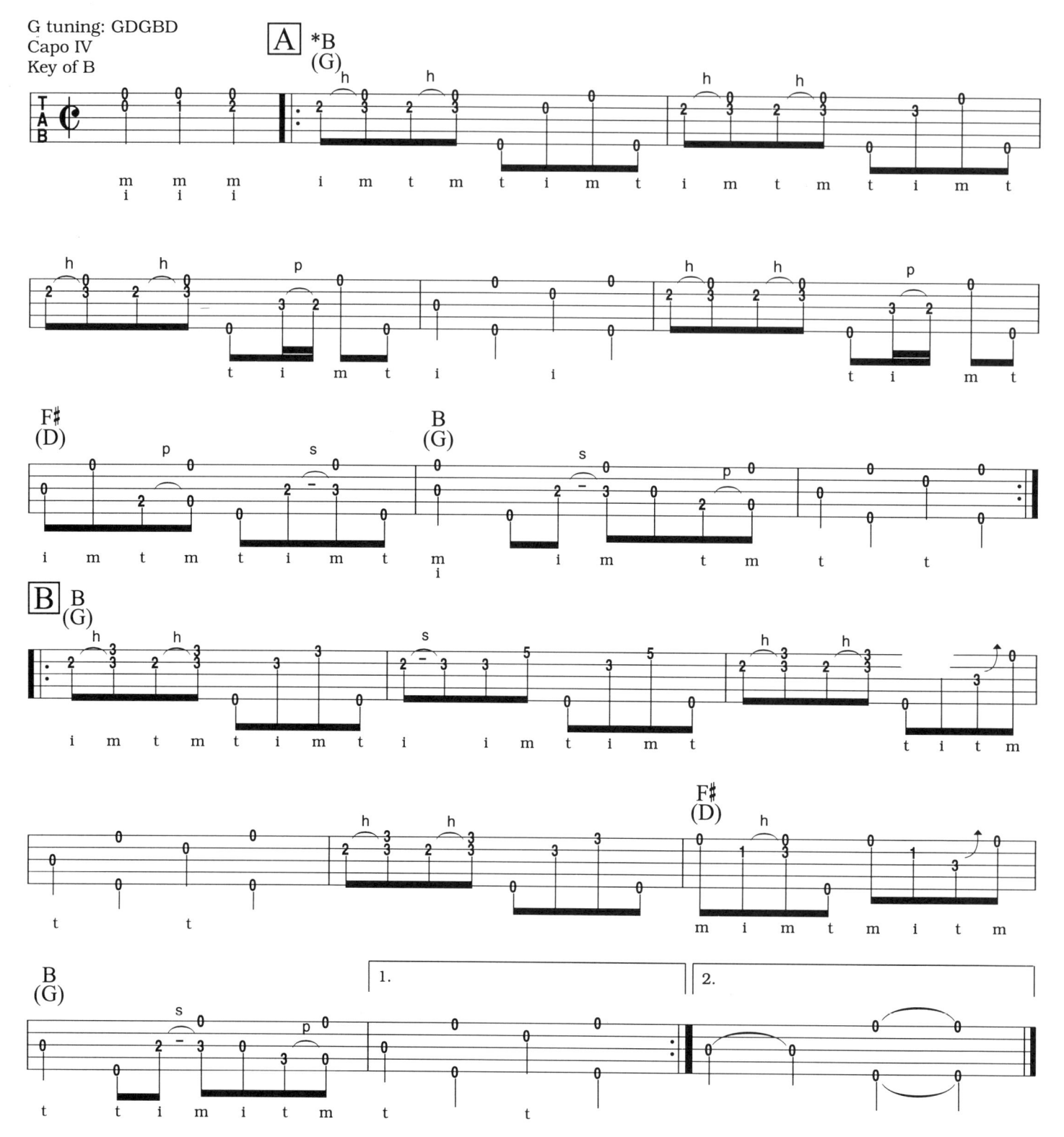

G tuning: GDGBD
Capo IV
Key of B

*Symbols in parentheses reflect chord names when no capo is used.

19 Here is the same music slowed down. We'll skip the repeats this time.

20 Let's capo at the fourth fret and play in the key of B. Hang on, we're going to play this fast!

Sally Johnson

G tuning: GDGBD
Key of G

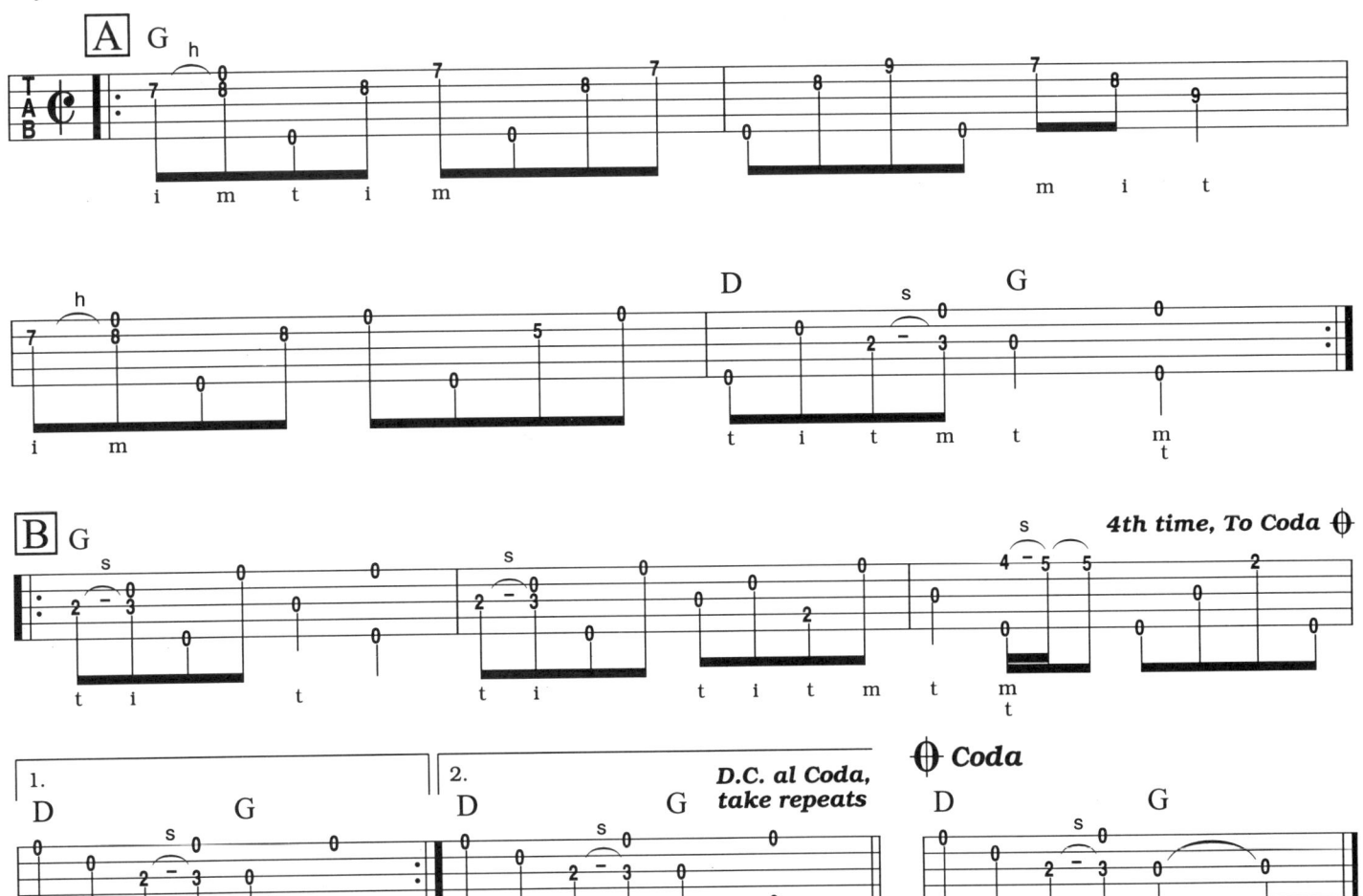

[sheet music tablature]

22 To begin, use the index finger of your left hand to hold the 7th fret of the second string and hammer-on with your middle finger to the 8th fret. Then move your index finger to the 7th fret of the first string while still holding the second string 8th fret with your middle finger. While maintaining the positioning of these two fingers, use your pinky to hold the 9th fret of the first string in the second measure. Then lift off your pinky, and place your ring finger on the 9th fret of the third string. This technique will make playing up the neck easier.

23 Now I'll play the A and B parts slowly, one time through.

Wildwood Flower

G tuning: GDGBD
Key of C

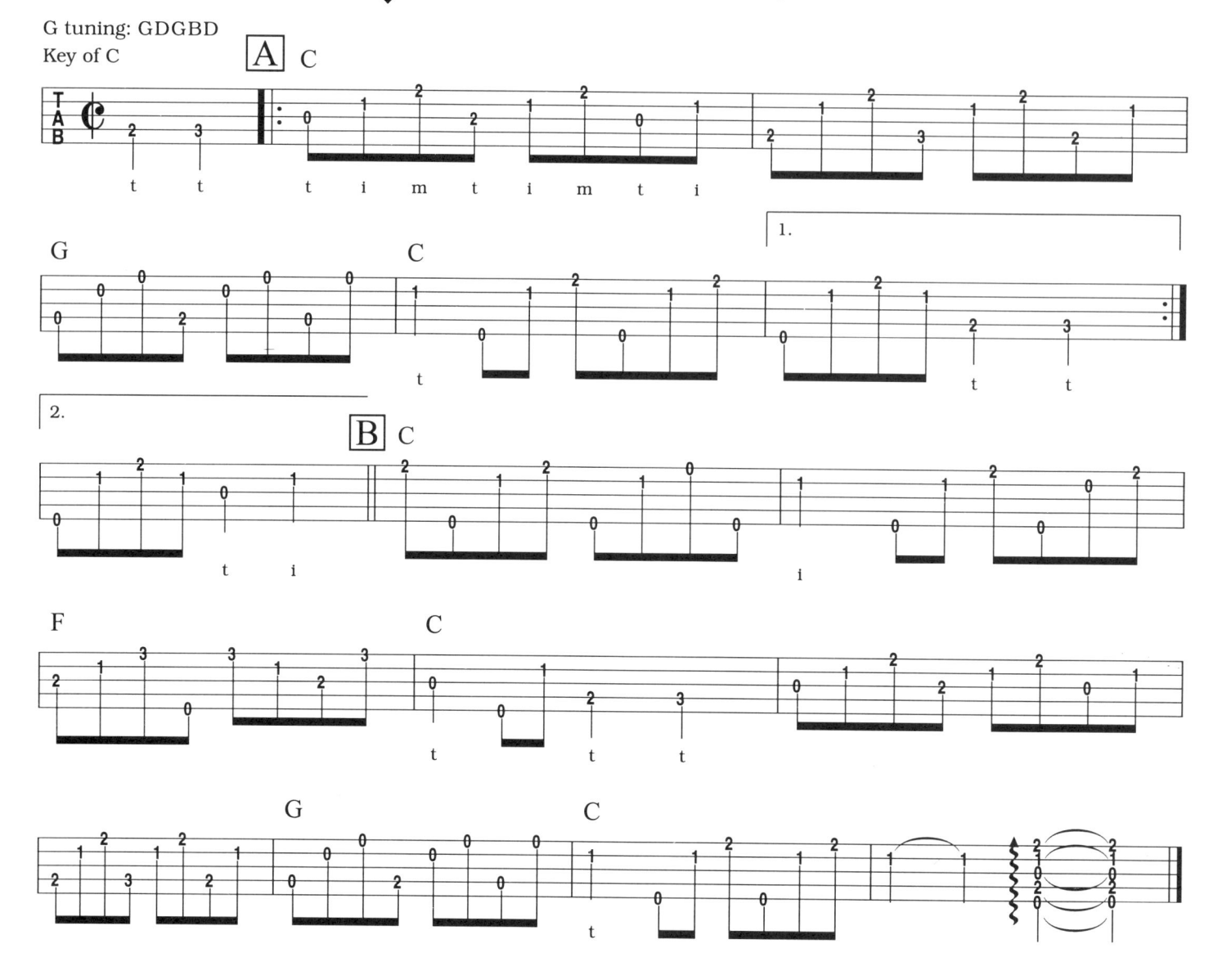

25 The trick to playing the A part of "Wildwood Flower" in C is to have all of your fingers of your left hand in proper position. Begin by holding down the standard C chord.

The first pickup note on the fourth string, 2nd fret is part of the C chord you are holding. Use your pinky to play the next note on the fourth string, 3rd fret. The first two full measures contain a series of forward rolls in the C position. Move your middle finger from the 2nd fret of the fourth string to the 2nd fret of the third string to begin the second forward roll. Move your middle finger back to the fourth string to start the next measure. Again, use your pinky to play the fourth string, 3rd fret to begin the fifth forward roll in the middle of the second full measure.

26 Let me play it slow so you can get a feel for it. This time I will end the tune by substituting the same pattern from the first ending in place of the last measure. This will provide us with our two pickup notes to take us back around to part A if you want to play another verse.

27. Roll In My Sweet Baby's Arms

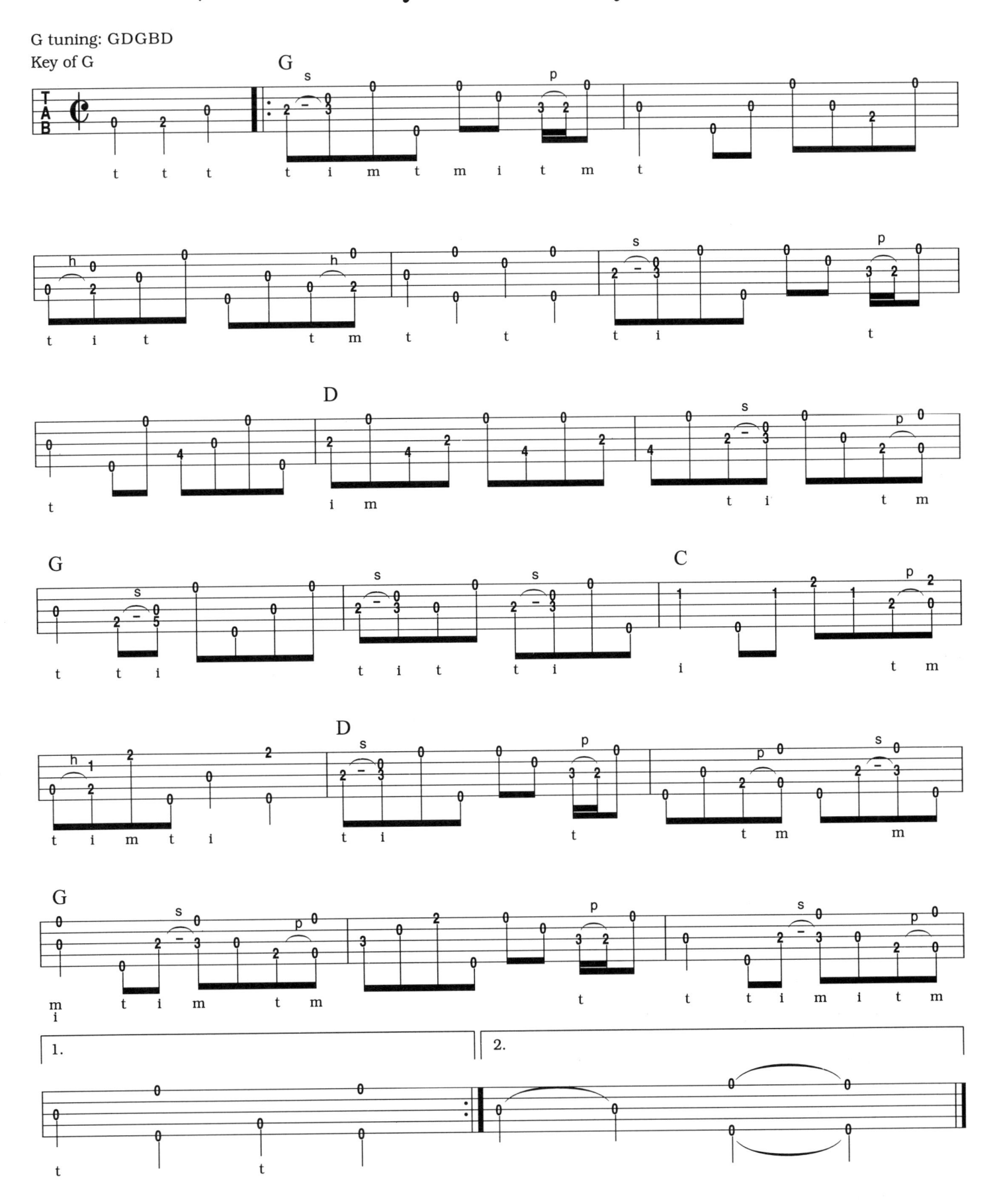

G tuning: GDGBD
Key of G

28. I'll play through this old standard again slow one time through and let you work through it. Notice that the last four measures are tag-endings in the style of Flatt and Scruggs.

11

29 For this fine old murder ballad we're going to tune our second string up a half-step to C to give it a lonesome modal sound.

Tuning:

① = D
② = C (up a half-step)
③ = G
④ = D
⑤ = G

Notice that the verse section is really the same melody and chord sequence as part A. I often ad lib during repeated verses. Here my part is written out for you to see the many possibilities for being creative. The ***D.S. al Coda*** marking at the end of the verse section sends you back to the 𝄋 sign. Continue to play through part A until you see ***To Coda*** ⊕. At that point, jump to the measure marked ***Coda*** ⊕ to end the song.

30 Pretty Polly

G tuning: GDGCD
Key of G

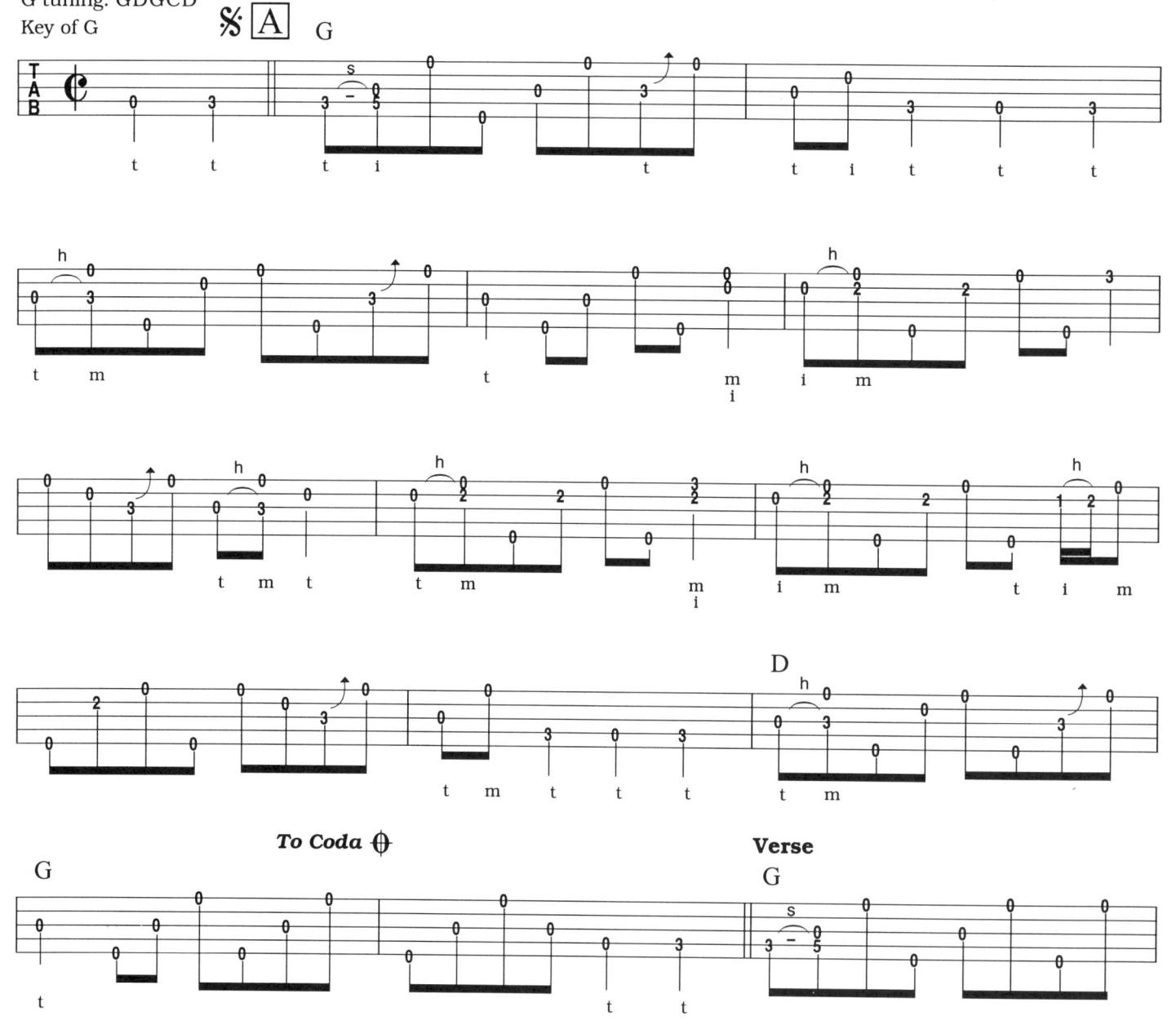

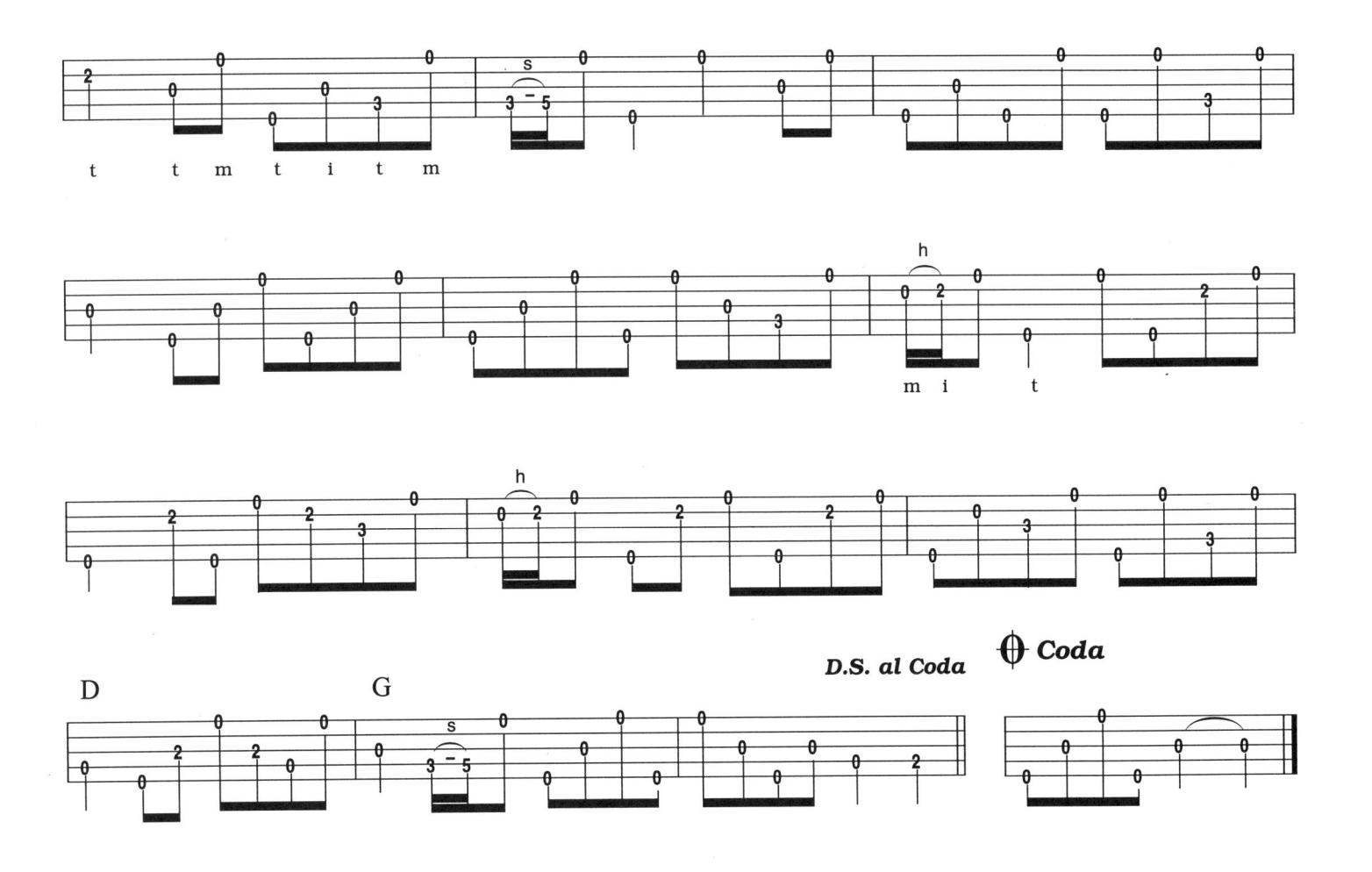

31 Notice how the chokes on the third string, 3rd fret give the tune that minor to major ambiguity that is so common in blues.

32 Now I'll play through part A slowly.

33 Nine Pound Hammer

G tuning: GDGBD
Key of G

[banjo tablature]

34
This tune is made up of a collection of Scruggs licks in which you slide up to, hammer-on, or pull-off to the melody note to embellish the tune.

35
Here's "Nine Pound Hammer" slowed down.

36
One nice lick is on the D chord in the second to the last line. It's basically a reworking of "Old Joe Clark" which is characterized by its accents on the off-beats.

37 Sitting on Top of the World

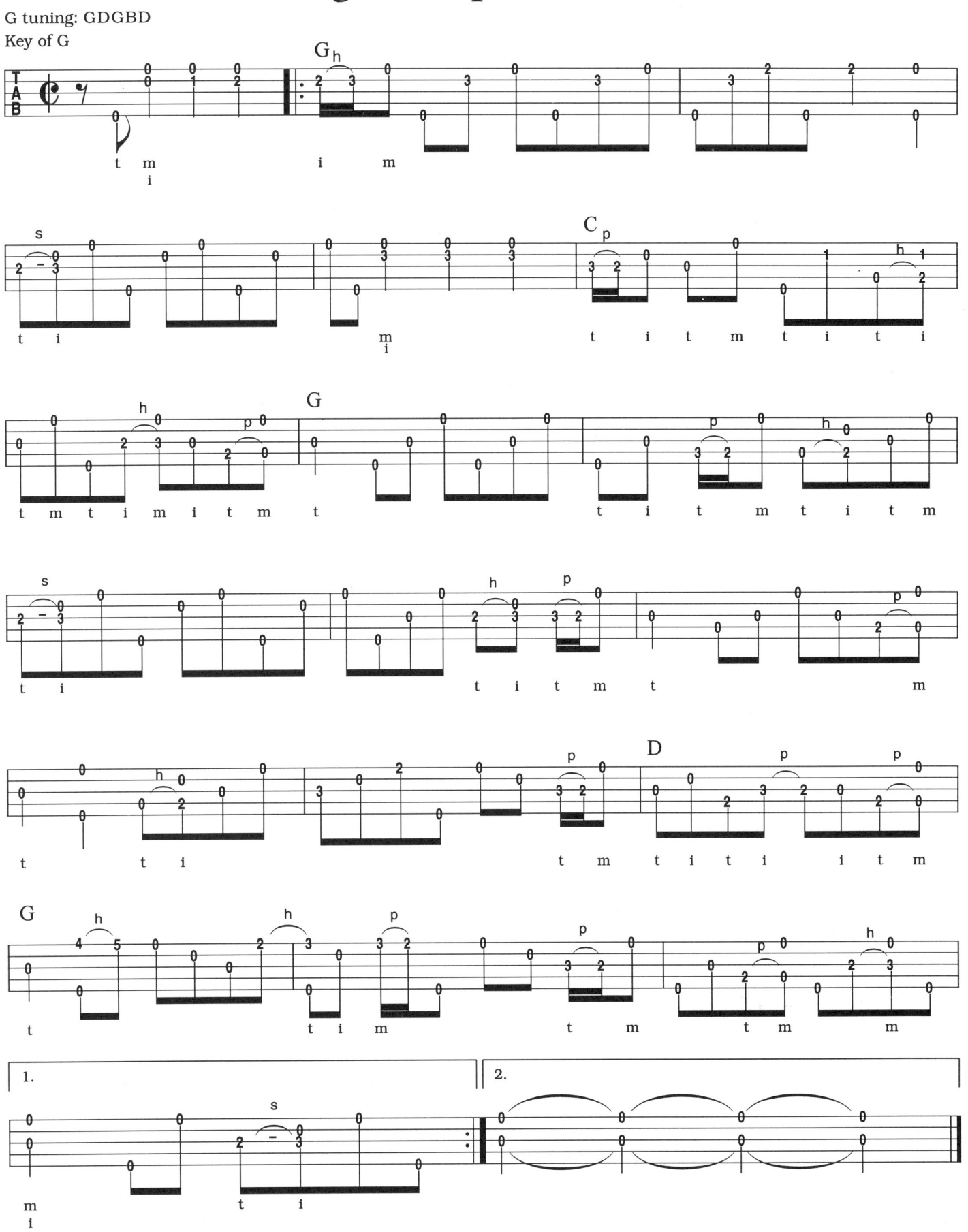

G tuning: GDGBD
Key of G

[Banjo tablature]

38 And here is the slow version.

39 Now let's examine some of the licks.

🔷40 John Henry

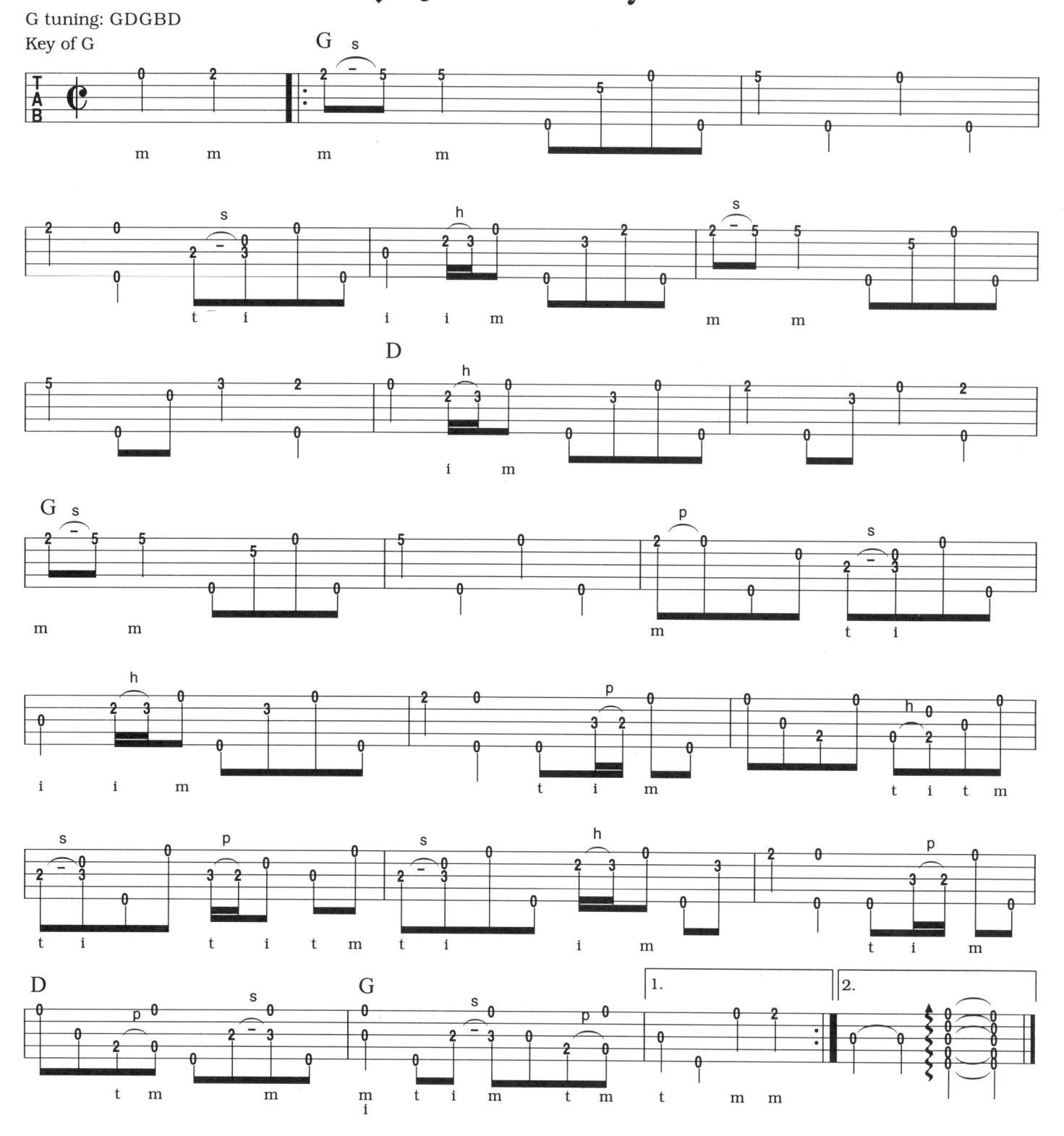

This is really one of my favorite tunes to play on the banjo. It starts out on the first string which gives it a nice drive.

🔷41

🔷42 Now I'll slow it down.

🔷43 There is a pull-off in the fourth line, third measure that is played slightly different than any of the pull-offs we have done so far. This is a slow pull-off which has the value of two eighth-notes. The first note is held with the first finger of your left hand. After you have picked the string, pull your finger downward off the fingerboard to give the second note a real nice snap.

Little Liza Jane

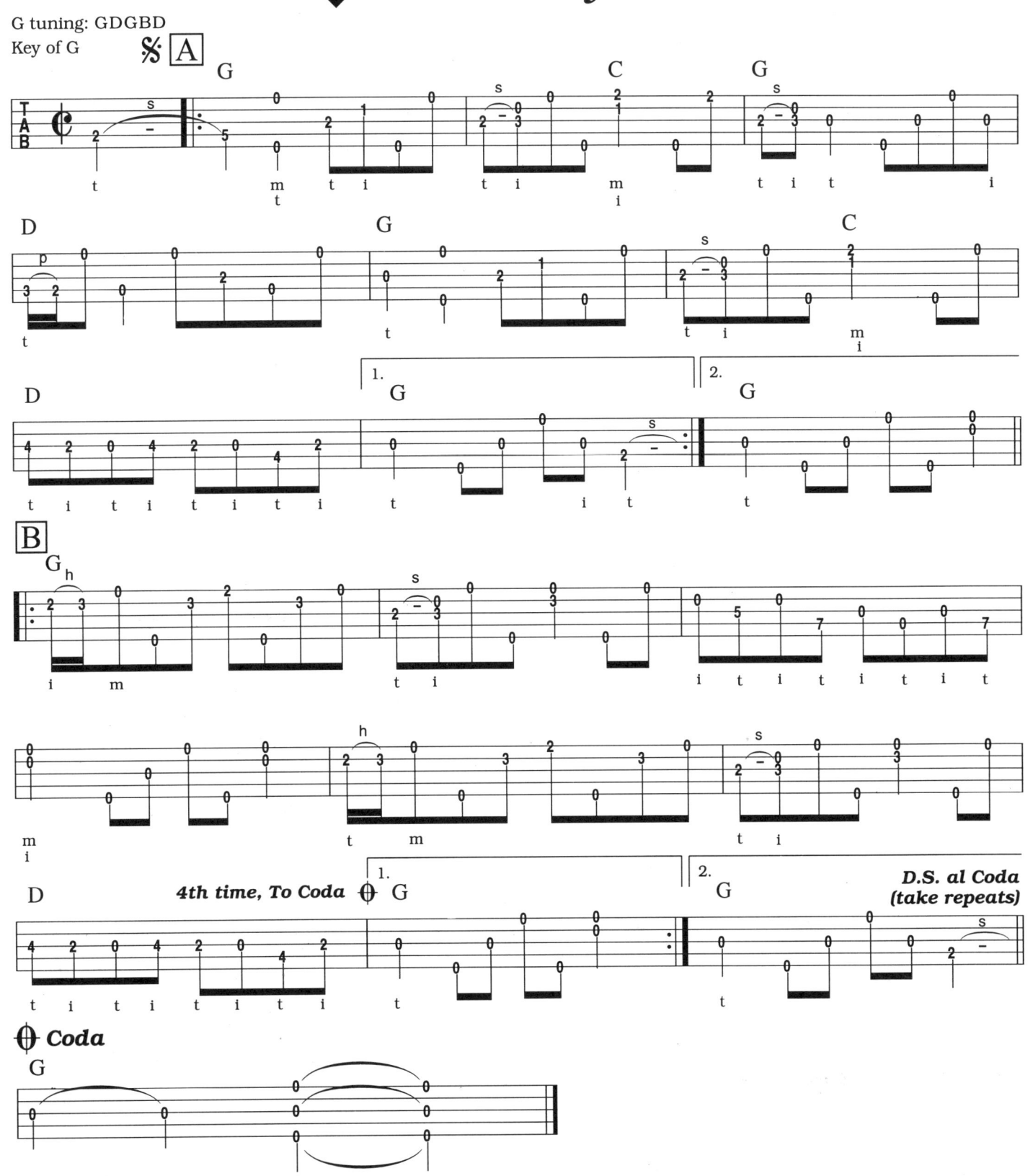

G tuning: GDGBD
Key of G

With "Little Liza Jane" we're getting into some new territory. Instead of only doing Scruggs-style licks, we're going to get into the single-string and melodic styles. The first measure of the third line is a Reno-style single-string lick. The melodic-style lick in this tune is located in the third measure of part B. The melodic-style, which consists of scalar patterns, is similar to the single-string style in that you can play note-for-note melodies, but the notes in the melodic-style are played on alternating strings.

Here's "Little Liza Jane" slowed down.

47 The last thing I want to mention before we go to the next tune is the pull-off that's at the beginning of the second line. Hold down the third fret with the middle finger and pull off to the index finger on the second fret. You can either push off your middle finger up towards the fifth string or pull down your middle finger towards the first string, as long as you get a good snap out of it.

48 Casey Jones

G tuning: GDGBD
Key of G

49 You may have noticed that I began to ad lib my part during the vocal repeat just as I did on the vocal section of "Pretty Polly." Here's your chance to be creative. Use your choice of rolls and work around the chords. Now let's analyze some of the new melodic licks from parts A and B.

Little Maggie

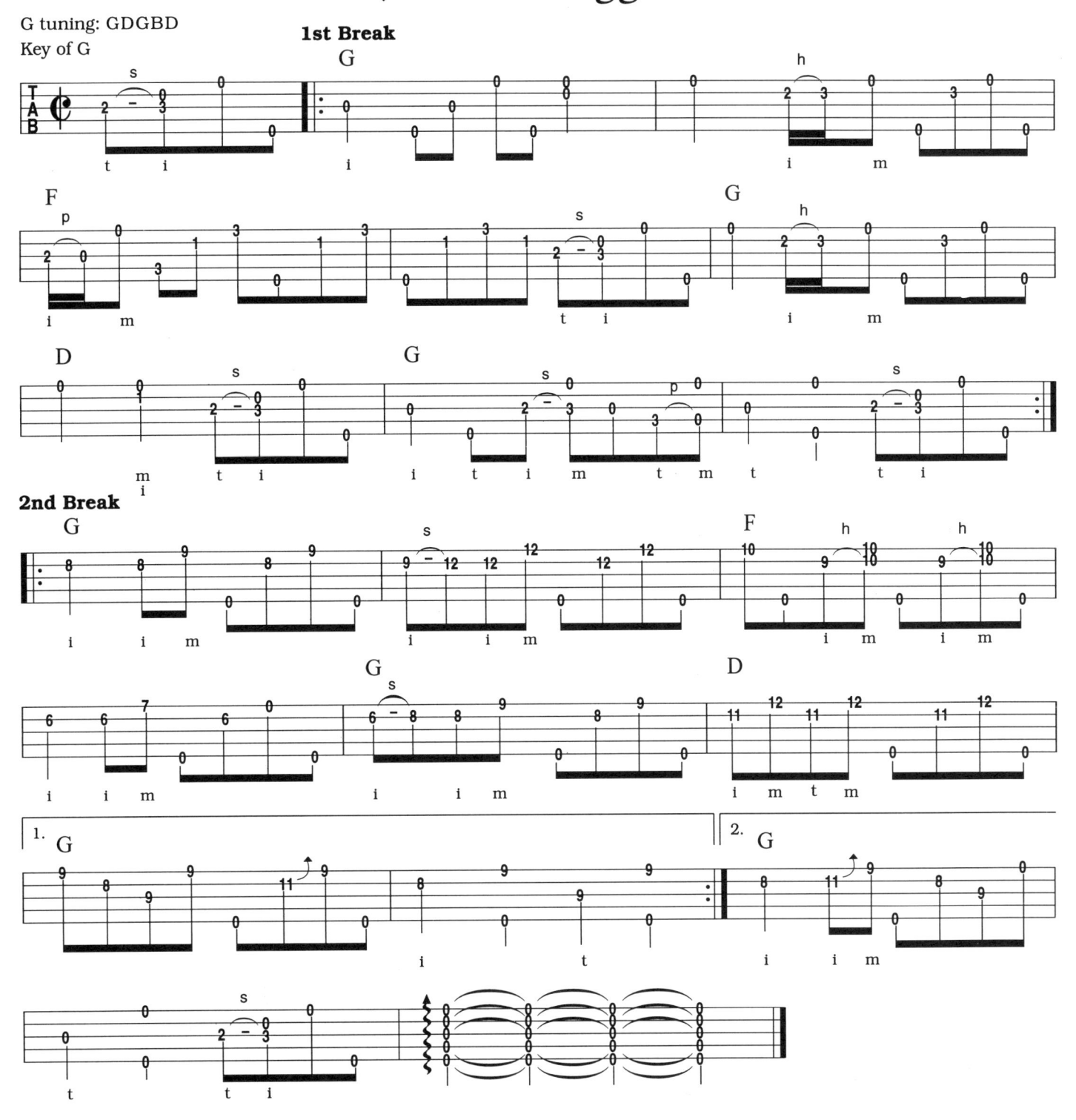

G tuning: GDGBD
Key of G

[Banjo tablature for "Little Maggie" — 1st Break (down the neck) and 2nd Break (up the neck), with chord symbols G, F, D above the staves and right-hand fingering indications (t, i, m) below.]

51 So, what we have here is two breaks, the first of which is down the neck and the second one is up the neck. When I wrote this version of "Little Maggie" I tried to follow the melody of the tune as closely as I could.

52 Let me slow it down and then we'll talk about it.

53 The down-the-neck break is fairly straight forward and the up-the-neck break is not that hard really. The first two lines in the 2nd break are played entirely on the first, second and fifth strings. The trick to these licks are to use your first finger of your left hand on the 8th fret of the second string and use your ring finger for the ninth fret of the 1st string. Then in the following measure, use your middle finger on the 9th fret of the second string to slide up to the 12th fret and again use your ring finger on the 12th fret of the first string. Then slide both your middle and ring fingers down to the 10th fret in the next measure. Now your first finger will be in position to hold down the 9th fret of the second string while using your middle finger to hammer on to the 10th fret. Throughout the rest of this break until the second measure of the second ending you'll want to use your middle finger for all of the notes on the second string, your ring finger for all of the notes on the first string and your first finger for all of the notes on the third string. The only exception is the 11th fret choked notes in the first measure of both the first and second endings which are fretted with the pinky.

🔷 54 Back Up and Push

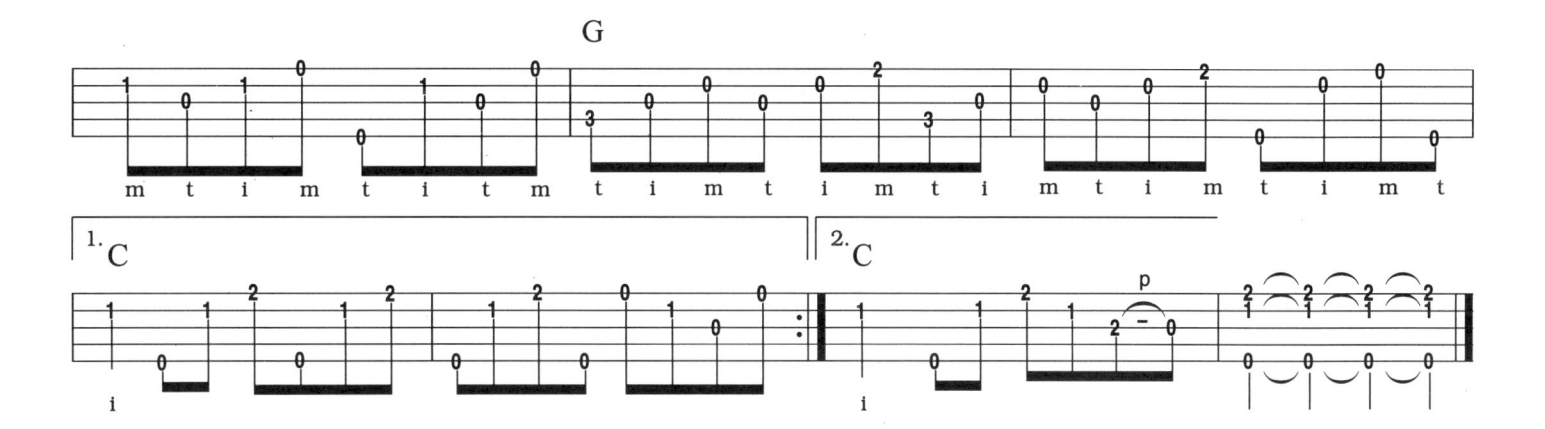

55 Now let's break down some of the licks and examine the fingerings.

56 Here's "Back Up and Push" slowed down. In this version, I've changed the second ending slightly to include pickup notes which will take you back to the 1st Break.

Here is the new second ending:

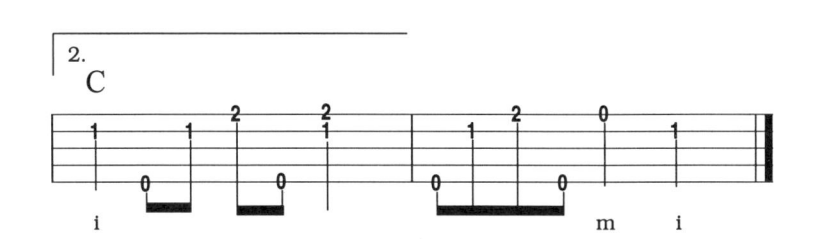

🎵 57 Red Wing

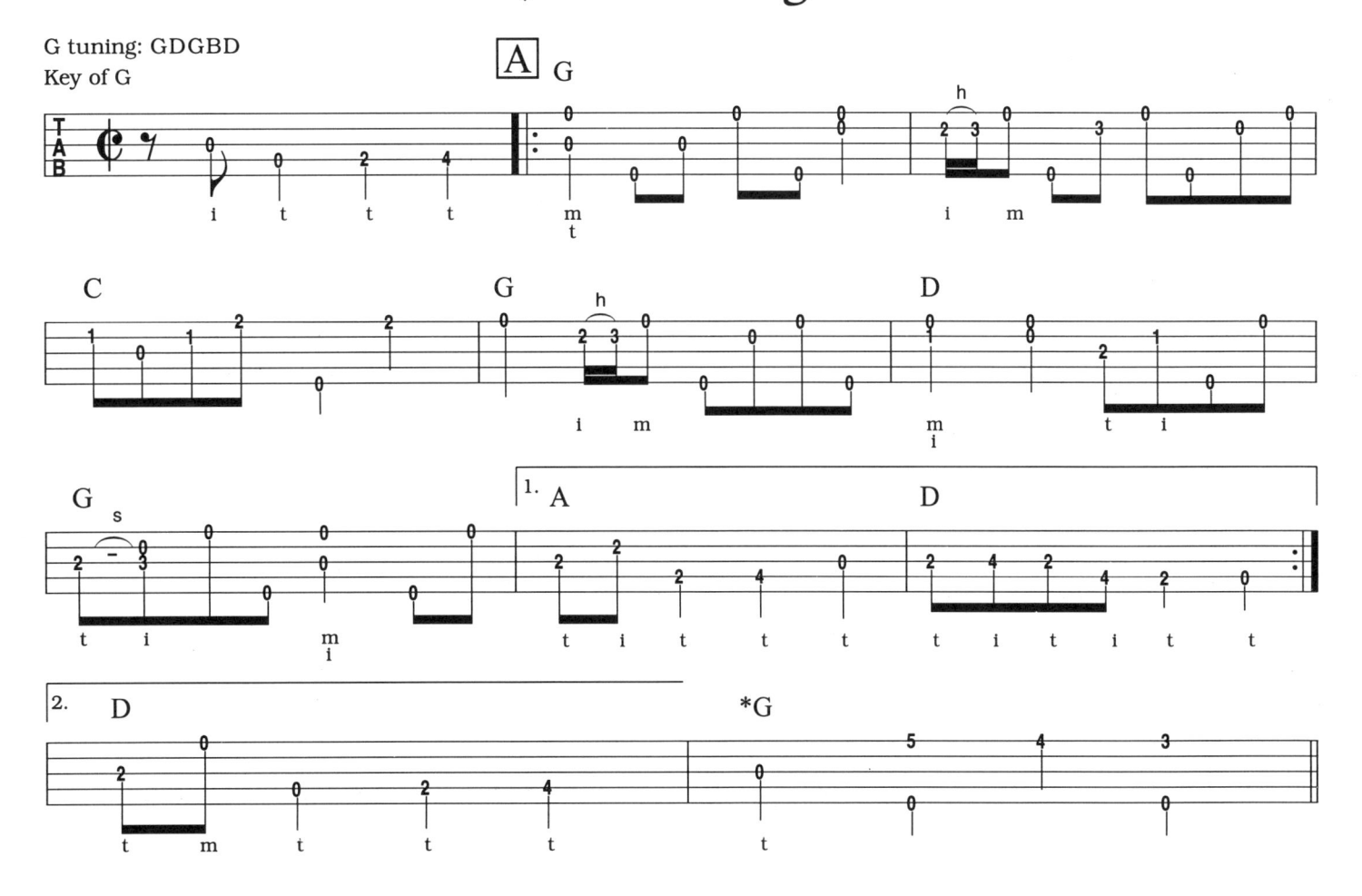

G tuning: GDGBD
Key of G

21

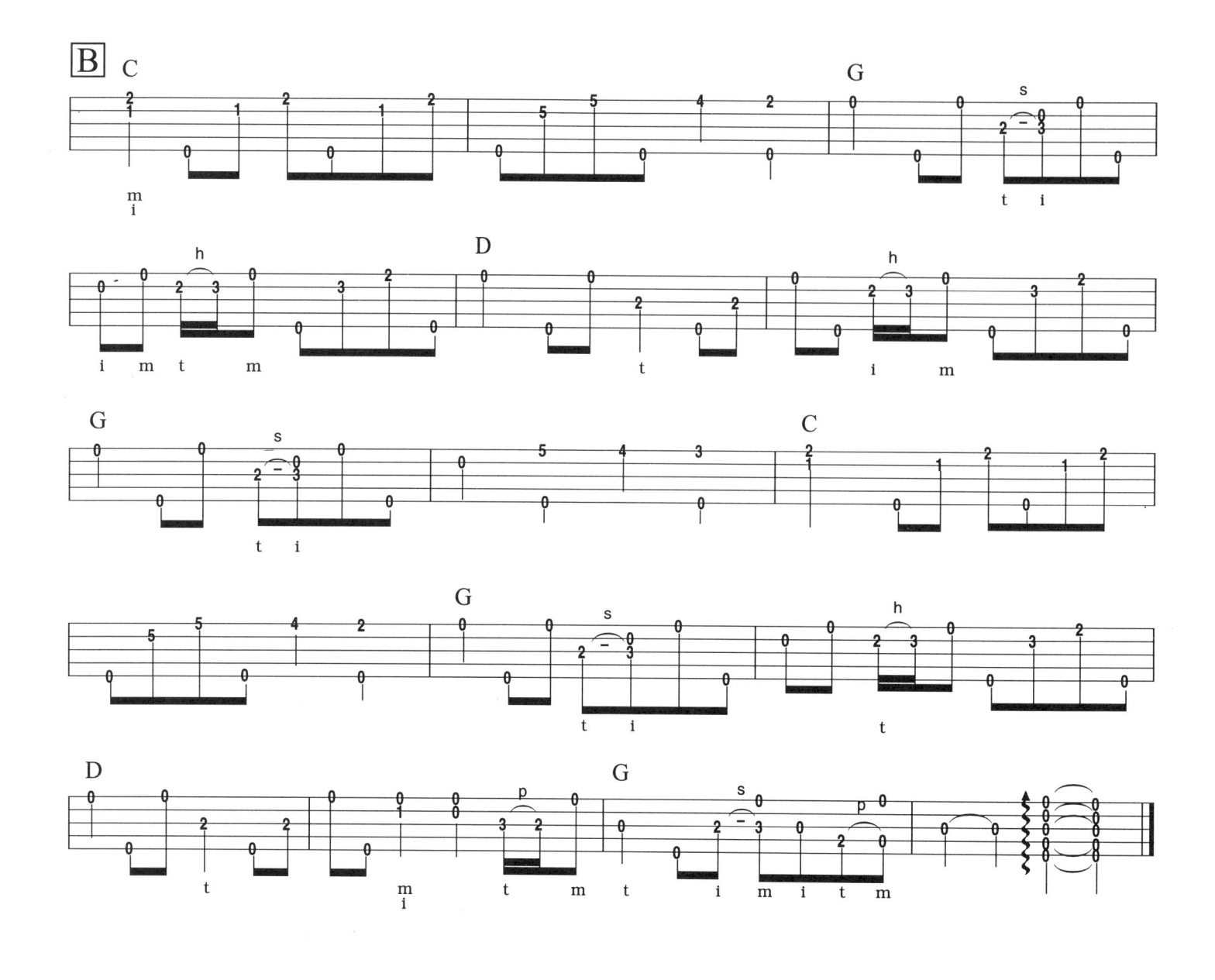

58 Let's look at the second measure of the third line; to play the A chord, barre your index finger across the 2nd fret of the second string.

At the bottom of the page is an alternate way to get from the second ending of the A part to the B part. The first measure of these substitute measures introduces contrary motion. While the notes on the first string descend in pitch, the notes on the third and second strings ascend.

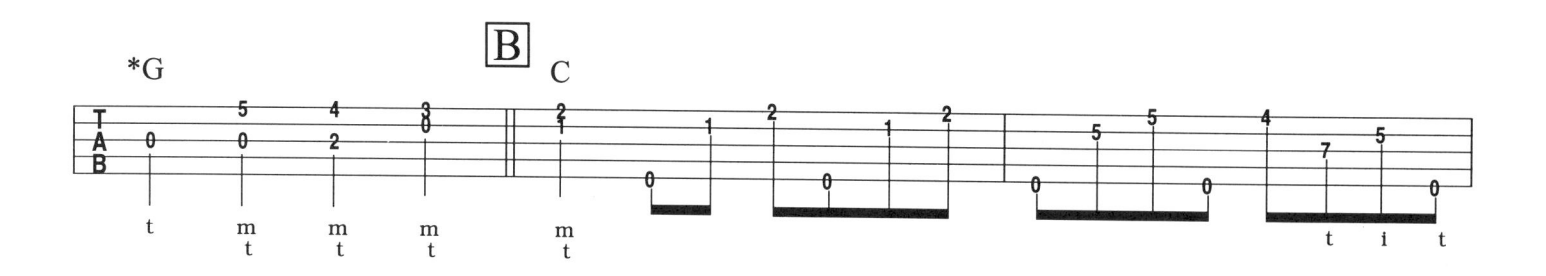

59 Here's the slow version of "Red Wing."

Little Rabbit

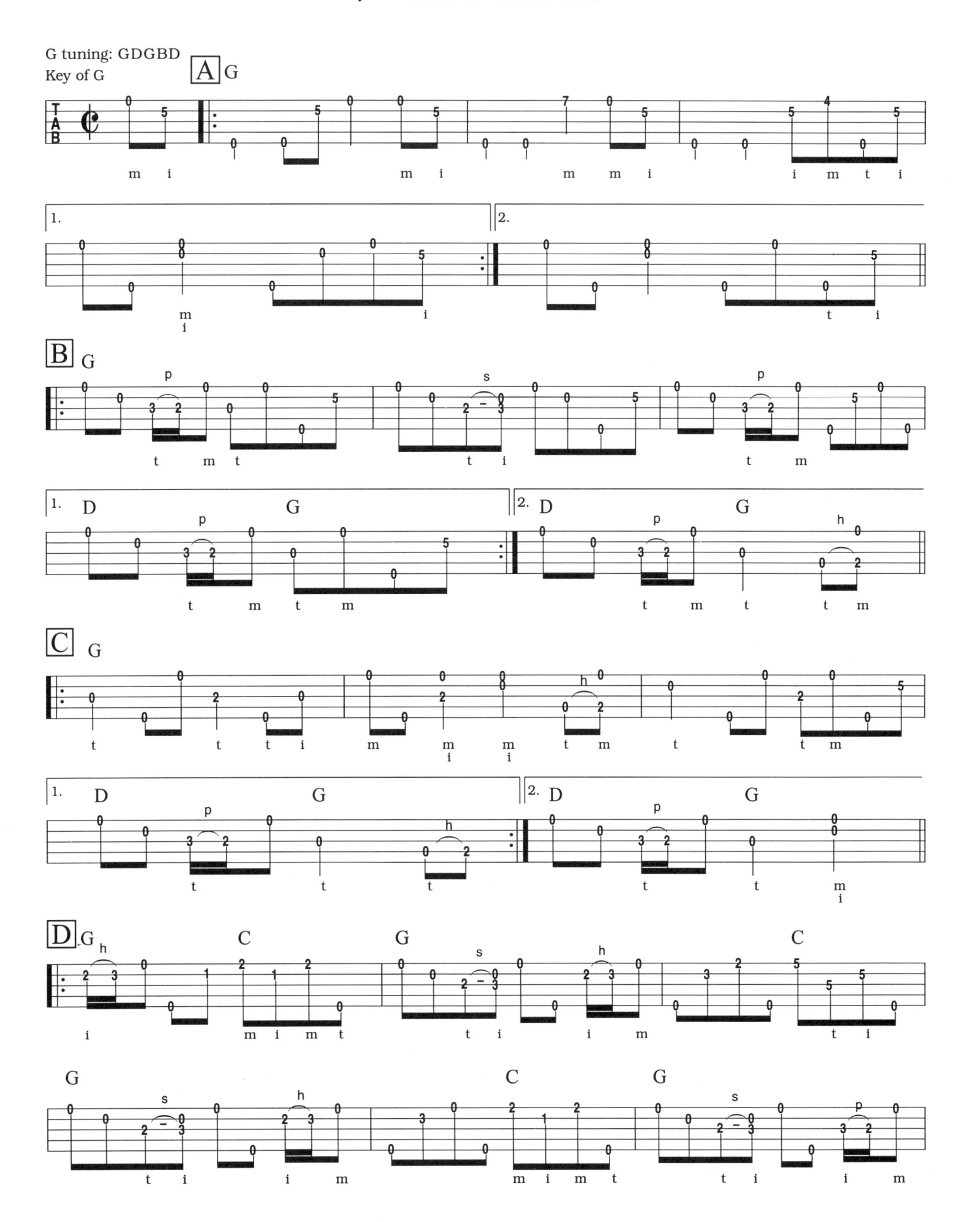

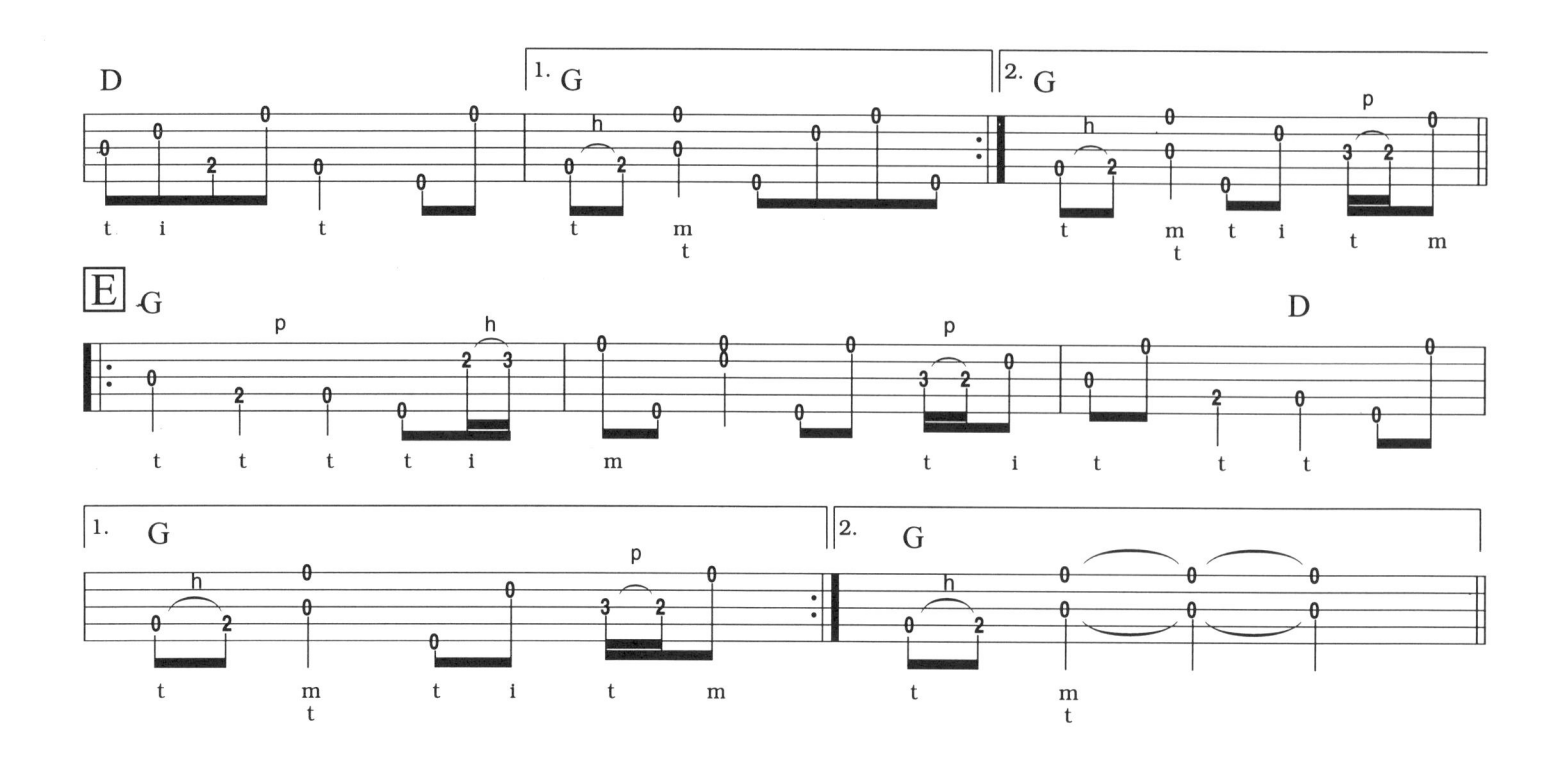

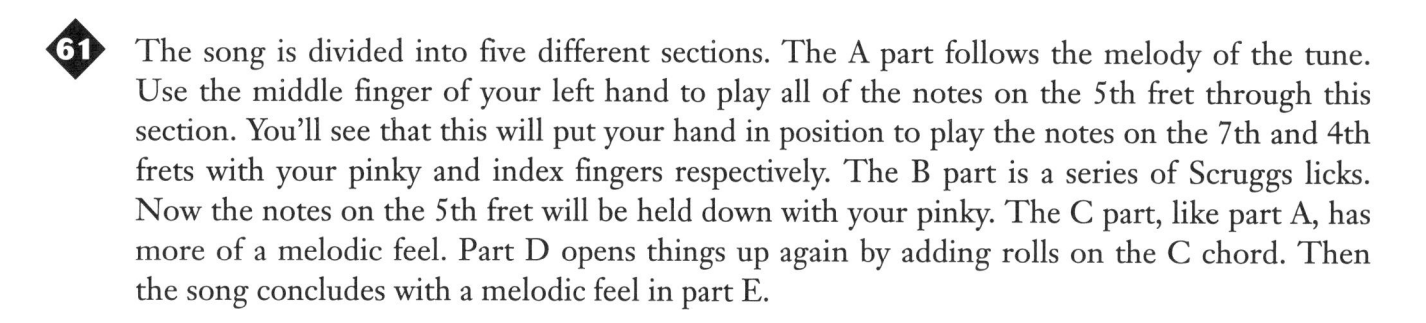

61 The song is divided into five different sections. The A part follows the melody of the tune. Use the middle finger of your left hand to play all of the notes on the 5th fret through this section. You'll see that this will put your hand in position to play the notes on the 7th and 4th frets with your pinky and index fingers respectively. The B part is a series of Scruggs licks. Now the notes on the 5th fret will be held down with your pinky. The C part, like part A, has more of a melodic feel. Part D opens things up again by adding rolls on the C chord. Then the song concludes with a melodic feel in part E.

62 So here's "Little Rabbit" again slowed down.

63 Uncle Joe

G tuning: GDGBD
Key of G

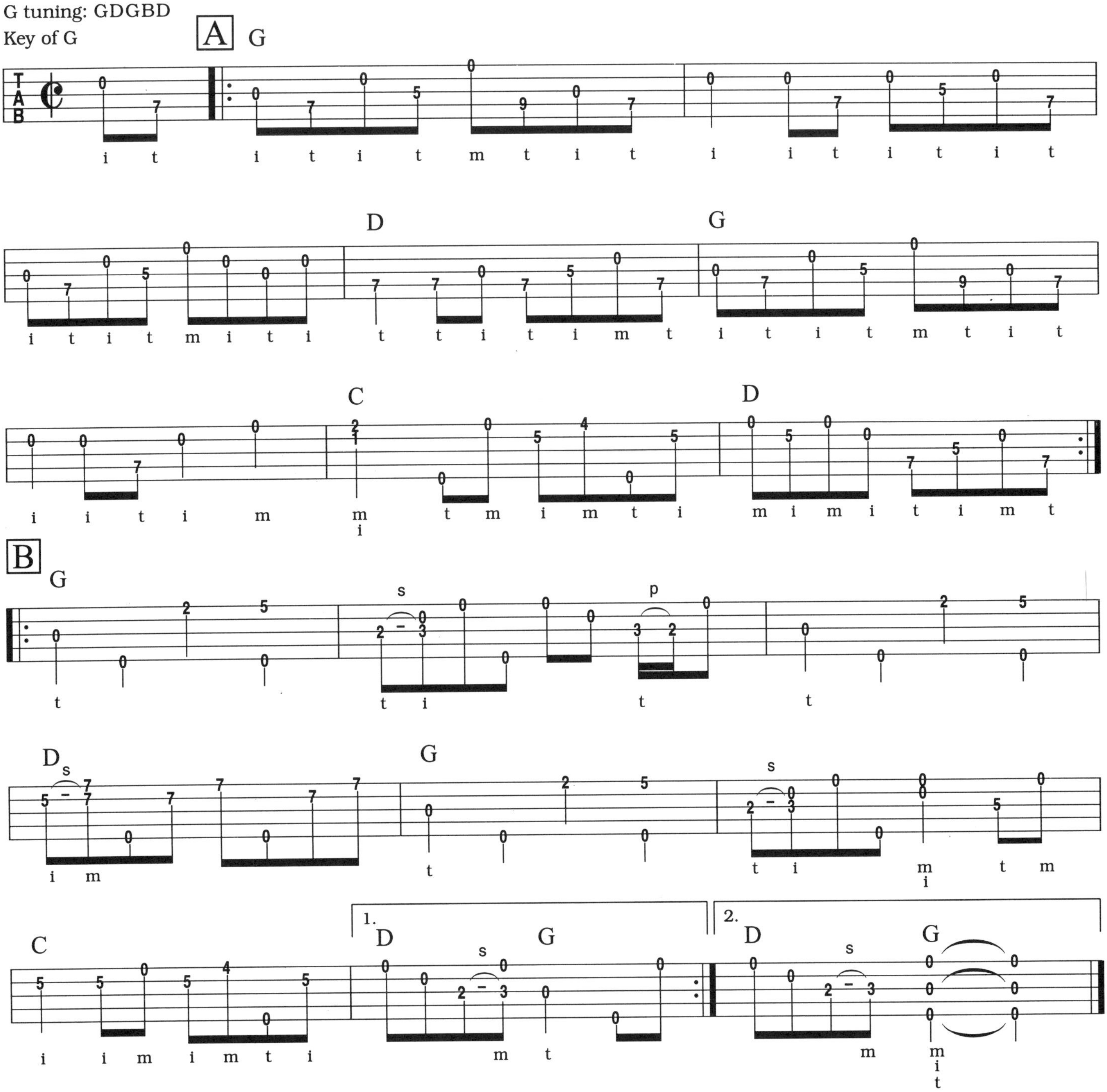

64 Watch out for the rhythms on this tune. I highly recommend using a metronome when you practice so that you develop a solid feel. Start out with the metronome on a slow setting. Only when you are able to play through the most difficult spots in the tune without faltering should you consider trying a faster tempo.

Alabama Jubilee

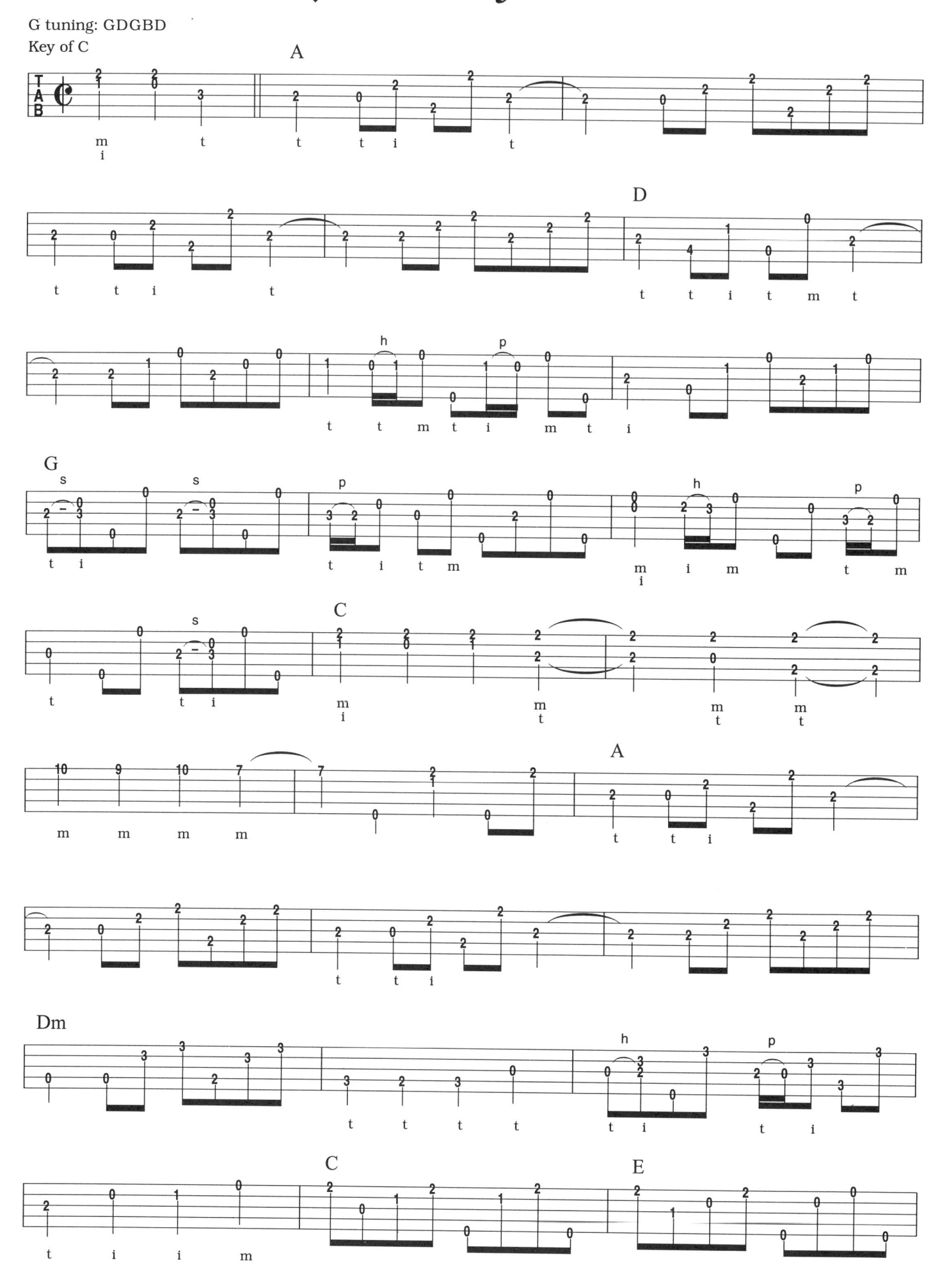

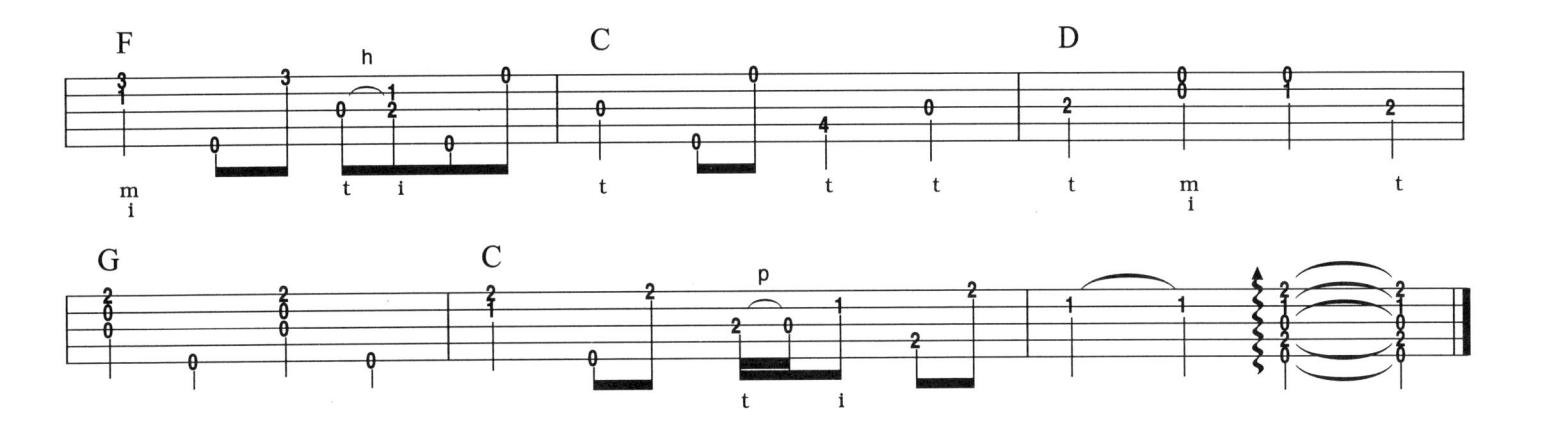

66 Now let's examine some of the more difficult areas and I'll explain the proper hand positions. Here are a few of the chords used:

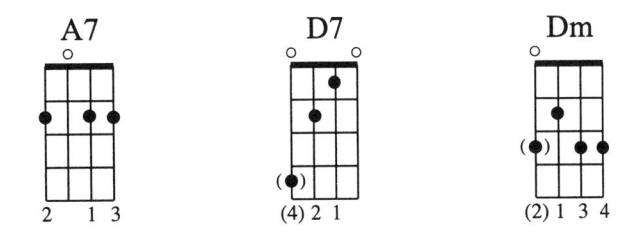

A7   D7   Dm

Here's an ending that will cap off the tune with style.

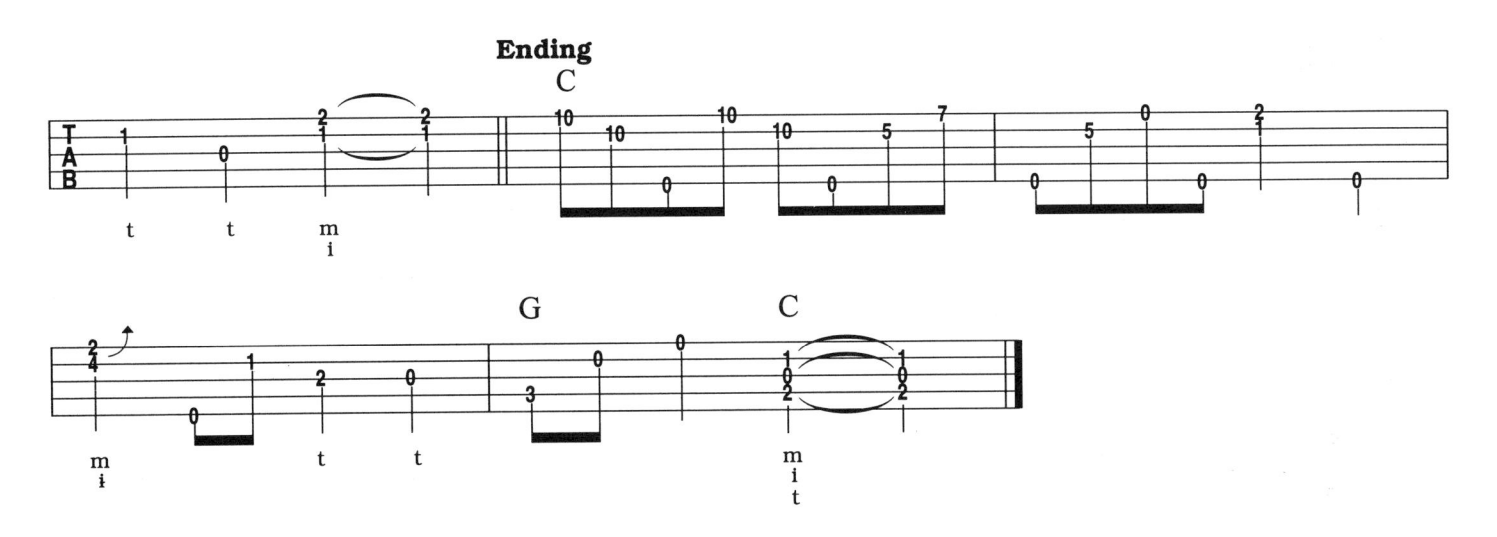

67 So here it is slowed down. We'll skip the last measure of the tune and go directly to the ending that we just examined.

Cumberland Gap

G tuning: F#DF#AD
Key of D

[Sheet music tablature for Cumberland Gap, with sections A and B, first and second endings, D.C. al Coda, Coda, and Ending]

D Tuning:

① = D
② = A (down a whole-step)
③ = F# (down a half-step)
④ = D
⑤ = F# (down a half-step)

Now let's see how D tuning works for "Cumberland Gap."

Here's the slow version. The second time through part B, skip the second ending and go directly to the Coda to end the tune.

Banjo Notation Legend

Each of the five horizontal lines below indicate a string of the banjo:

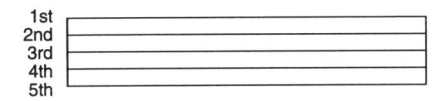

The numbers placed on the lines represent the frets to be fingered. For instance, here you'll be playing the third fret of the second string:

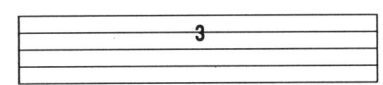

As a basic unit of measure I'll be using eight eighth-notes per measure. Notice that eighth-notes have a beam joining the descending stems when two or more are consecutive. A stem with a flag is used for single eighth notes:

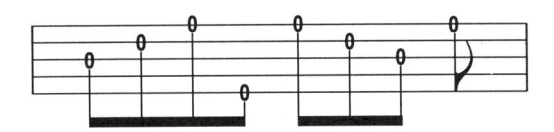

In just about every tune there will be at least a couple of sixteenth notes sprinkled amongst the eighths. One sixteenth note has half the time value of an eighth note and is indicated by two beams when connected with another sixteenth:

You'll also come across quarter notes. These have the time value of two eighth notes and are indicated by a single descending stem:

Periods of silence, called rests, are indicated using standard music notation symbols. They are of the same duration as their corresponding note:

eighth rest   quarter rest

Right hand fingerings appear beneath the notes as follows:

t = thumb   i = index   m = middle

Left hand moves will have these designations:

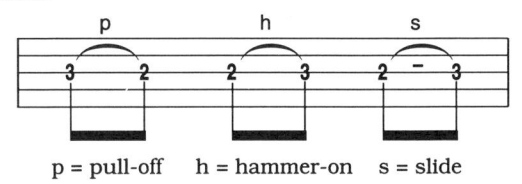

p = pull-off   h = hammer-on   s = slide

A choked note will be represented by a curved arrow:

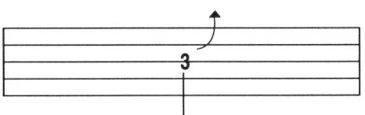

A note that is choked, held in that position and then released will warrant the following symbol (see "Cumberland Gap"):

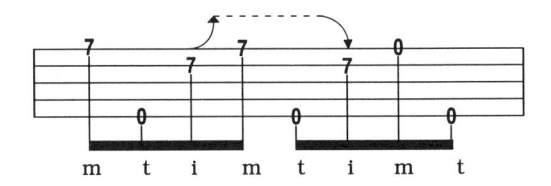

When you find an arching line between two notes, you should play only the first note and let it ring through the time value of the second:

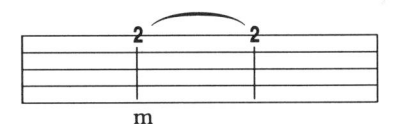

Repeat signs are common and usually apply to an entire section (part A or part B) of a tune. These signs appear at each end of the material to be repeated:

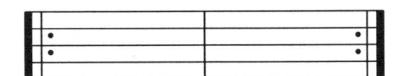

In cases where repeated material has two different endings, you'll see the following marking. Here, you'll play the section to be repeated through the first ending. Then you'll play the section again, this time skipping the first ending and playing the second:

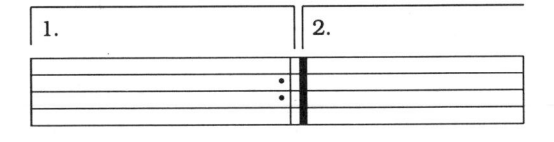

29

A Selected Discography

Solo Recordings (Rounder)

Glory Shone Around: A Christmas Collection	1995
(*1996 NAIRD Nominee for Best Album in a Seasonal Category)	
World Turning	1993
Solo Banjo Works with Béla Fleck	1993
Rounder Banjo Extravaganza	1992
Dust on the Needle	1988
Hill Country	1985
Robot Plane Flies over Arkansas	1983
Fiddle Tunes for Banjo (w/Béla Fleck & Bill Keith)	1981
Banjoland	1976
Heartlands	1975
Bluegrass Light	1974

With Skyline (Flying Fish)

Fire of Grace	1989
Skyline Drive	1986
Stranded in the Moonlight	1984
Late to Work	1983

With Country Cooking (Rounder)

Country Cooking (compilation)	1989
Barrel of Fun	1974
Frank Wakefield	1972
15 Bluegrass Instrumentals	1971

With Psychograss

Like Minds (Sugar Hill)	1996
Psychograss (Windham Hill)	1994

Continue Your Studies With Tony Trischka

If you have enjoyed this instructional CD and book, Tony has produced additional bluegrass banjo lessons for Homespun Tapes.

Video
Bluegrass Banjo Tunes and Techniques
   taught by Tony Trischka
   with guests David Grier (guitar)
   and Andrea Zonn (fiddle)
   90-min. video with tab + practice tape $39.95

Audio
Hot Licks For Bluegrass Banjo
   taught by Tony Trischka
   Two audio cassettes $28.00
   Two audio cassettes with 144-page book $45.95

The Advanced Banjo Workshop
   taught by Bill Keith and Tony Trischka
   Six audio cassettes with tab $49.95

- Tony Trischka originally recorded Easy Banjo Solos for Homespun Tapes as one audio cassette with tab. We have digitally-remastered and edited this popular instructional tape to create this Listen & Learn publication.

These and hundreds of other top instructional tapes are available from your music dealer or directly from Homespun Tapes. For complete catalog, write or call:

Homespun Tapes

Box 694 • Woodstock, NY 12498 • (800) 33-TAPES

Homespun Listen & Learn Series

This exciting new series features lessons from the top pros with in-depth CD instruction and thorough accompanying booklet.

GUITAR

Tony Rice Teaches Bluegrass Guitar*
A Master Picker Analyzes His Pioneering Licks And Solos
Tony Rice is known world-wide for his spectacular technique, brilliant improvisation and powerful soloing. In this lesson, he personally passes on to you the style he has developed during the two decades as the top bluegrass flatpicker of his generation. In careful detail, Tony analyzes licks, runs, solos and rhythm parts to hot bluegrass songs and fiddle tunes that will challenge and delight all flatpickers. Before long you'll be picking solos to the following essential bluegrass tunes: "The Red Haired Boy," "Little Sadie," "Your Love Is Like A Flower," "Blue Railroad Train," "Home From The Forest," "Wildwood Flower," "Old Train," "Wild Horse," and "Jerusalem's Ridge."
_____00695045 Book/CD Pack.....................$19.95

Happy Traum Teaches Blues Guitar*
A Hands-On Beginner's Course In Acoustic Country Blues
Take a lesson in fingerstyle blues guitar from one of the world's most respected teacher/performers. All you need to know is how to play a few basic chords to get started playing along with this user-friendly book/audio package. Beginning with the most basic strumming of a 12-bar blues pattern. Happy gradually starts adding fills, runs, turnarounds, bass rhythms and "boogie woogie" walking bass patterns that make the basic blues progression come alive. All of these elements are notated in both notes and tab.
_____00841082 Book/CD Pack.....................$19.95

Richard Thompson Teaches Traditional Guitar Instrumentals*
A Legendary Guitarist Teaches His Unique Arrangements To Irish, Scottish and English Tunes
Learn the techniques and style of traditional Irish, English and Scottish jigs, reels, hornpipes and other tunes arranged for fingerstyle guitar. On the CD, Richard explains how he uses altered tunings, string bends, vibrato as well as other techniques to give these tunes added "flavor." The book contains all of the songs and techniques written in notation and tab.
_____00841083 Book/CD Pack.....................$19.95

PIANO

David Cohen Teaches Blues Piano
A Hands-On Beginner's Course In Traditional Blues
Sit down at the piano and start to boogie. This easy play along course will have you rockin' and rollin' in no time – even if you have never played blues piano before. David Cohen (The Blues Project, Country Joe and the Fish, etc.) starts you at the beginning, quickly getting you into the elementary theory needed to understand chord progressions and the 12-bar blues form. Then it's right into setting up a solid left-hand rhythm in the bass to create a bedrock for the right hand improvisations to come. By the time this lesson ends, you'll be jamming the blues, plus you'll have a solid foundation on which to build.
_____00841084 Book/CD Pack.....................$19.95

HARMONICA

John Sebastian Teaches Blues Harmonica
A Complete Guide For Beginners
A rock 'n' roll legend teaches you everything you need to play great blues harp in this unique lesson. John Sebastian starts at the beginning, carefully explaining the proper way to hold the instrument and make your first tones. John explains and demonstrates essential techniques such as reed bending, vibrato, rhythm grooves, "cross harp" playing and more as well as several great blues licks and complete solos. Lessons are written in notation and tablature.
_____00841074 Book/CD Pack.....................$19.95

PENNYWHISTLE

Cathal McConnell Teaches Irish Pennywhistle
A Hands-On Beginner's Course In Traditional Irish Repertoire And Technique
Learn to play traditional Irish songs on an instrument the whole family can enjoy. Cathal McConnell, known world-wide for his work with the popular Celtic band Boys of the Lough, teaches you the basics from the proper way to hold and blow the whistle, to the slurs, trills, rolls and other important techniques that will give you a truly Irish "feel." 12 traditional Irish folksongs are notated and explained in detail. As a bonus, the guitar accompaniment is recorded on one stereo channel while the pennywhistle is recorded on the other, so you can play along with only the accompaniment when you have mastered each tune.
_____00841081 Book/CD Pack.....................$19.95

For more information, see your local music dealer, or write to:

HAL•LEONARD CORPORATION
7777 W. Bluemound Rd. P.O. Box 13819 Milwaukee, WI 53213

*Contains tablature